Bluffers

GUIDE TO

WINE

JONATHAN GOODALL AND HARRY EYRES

© Haynes Publishing 2018
Published June 2018
Reprinted November 2018

A CIP Catalogue record for this book
is available from the British Library.

ISBN: 978 1 78521 241 3 (print)
      978 1 78521 554 4 (eBook)

Library of Congress control no. 2018932884

Published by Haynes Publishing,
Sparkford, Yeovil, Somerset BA22 7JJ
Tel: 01963 440635
Int. tel: +44 1963 440635
Website: www.haynes.com

Printed in Malaysia.

Series Editor: David Allsop.
Front cover illustration by Alan Capel.

CONTENTS

ß

This guide will give you the tools to persuade marvelling listeners that you are a connoisseur of rare ability and experience – without anybody discovering that, until you read it, all you really knew about wine was that it's red, white or somewhere in between.

IN VINO VERITAS

Wine has a mystique like no other drink and few other subjects. Many people are often defeated by it, thinking that in order to claim any knowledge of it they need to have visited various vineyards in France, to have a cellar (i.e., not a cupboard under the stairs), or to be able to identify exactly where a wine comes from without looking at the label.

This, needless to say, is nonsense. Long gone are the days when the wine drinker would ignore anything that didn't come from France or Germany. New World wine countries – Australia, New Zealand, the USA, Chile, Argentina and South Africa – have put themselves firmly on the map. Sleeping giants like Italy, Spain and Portugal are realising their potential with new and exciting styles. Even Greek wine, once a lost cause, has improved. The grapevine, in fact, is being cultivated in the most implausible places, from the hills of Maharashtra to the paddy-fields of Thailand and even the sheep-filled wilderness of Patagonia. And with global warming gathering pace, Falkland Islands

Cabernet Franc and Greenland Gewürztraminer may not be far off. The message to the bluffer, then, is not to be intimidated by the mystique.

Some familiarity with the old traditions and etiquette is desirable, however, so that you can take on the *bon viveur* at his or her own game. This guide sets out to conduct you through the main danger zones in which you are most likely to encounter wine and the wine expert, and to equip you with a vocabulary and an evasive technique that will minimise the risk of being rumbled as a bluffer.

But it will do more. It will give you the tools to persuade legions of marvelling listeners that you are a connoisseur of rare ability and experience – without anybody discovering that, until you read it, all you really knew about wine was that it's red, white or somewhere in between.

THE BASICS

Put in the most simple terms, wine is fermented grape juice. People may make, talk about and even drink elderflower wine, peach wine, kiwi-fruit wine or whatever, but as a wine bluffer you do not need to know about them. And on no account discuss them. These fermented fruit concoctions have no mystique, and thus no bluffing potential.

Non-alcoholic wines are *not* wines. Wines, like some human beings, have an absolute need to be alcoholic. And they are made from grapes – and only grapes.

COLOUR

Wine comes in three basic colours: red, white and rosé. To look like a pro, tilt the glass slightly away from you so that you can look through the edge of the wine where it touches the glass. This can give the most telling indication of hue, and therefore age. To look like a *poseur,* tilt the glass in front of a white background, such as a piece of paper. The best way to assess a wine's 'brightness' (intensity of colour) is to look down through the glass.

Red Ranges from purple to light brown. A bright, intense colour is an indication of youthfulness and, occasionally, higher acidity. Young wines tend to be bright all the way to the edge, but the colour fades at the edge, gradually turning brown, as the wine ages. Old reds often have a pale, brick-red colour. Colour is also determined by the grape variety and, more specifically, by the thickness of the grape skins, where the pigments are found. For example, thick-skinned Cabernet Sauvignon or Syrah grapes produce darker, perhaps purple, wines; thin-skinned Pinot Noir might be a lighter cherry-red.

White Ranges from practically colourless through to pale green, straw-coloured, pale copper and deep gold to amber. Generally, very pale colours indicate a light, dry, unoaked wine, while deepening hues imply richer styles, possibly oaked and maybe sweeter. Colours usually deepen as the wine ages.

Rosé Ranges from the insipid pale-pink of so-called 'blush' wines from the USA, which taste as candy-like and confected as they look, to the bolder, deeper shades of metrosexual rosés from places like Navarra in Spain and Tavel in France's southern Rhône region.

SWEET AND DRY

First, it's as well to remember that anything calling itself 'medium' is, in fact, sweet. Second, all wines (except those made from grapes affected by 'noble rot'; *see* 'Botrytis' on page 149) are naturally dry. The sweetness comes either from stopping the fermentation before all the sugar has been converted to alcohol, or from adding unfermented grape juice, or from adding sugar, usually in liquid form.

All this doesn't mean you should scorn sweet wines. The ignorant have turned up their noses at them for so long that a very rewarding bluffing line can be cultivated in, say, the little-known sweet white wines of the Loire, or the really fine German Auslesen, Beerenauslesen and Trockenbeerenauslesen. It is a relief to know that the last two can be shortened to BA and TBA, respectively. If you want to create a real frisson, then recommend an Austrian TBA from a place called Rust.

FORTIFICATION

Most wines are unfortified – that is to say, they have only the alcohol provided by God in the form of sun and grapes. But some wines, like Port, Sherry, Madeira and the two venerable old white wines, Marsala and Malaga, are strengthened by the addition of anything from brandy to industrial alcohol. Fortified wines, like fortified towns, should not be taken lightly. They get you buzzing more quickly but can land you with the most appalling after-effects if you're not careful.

STILL OR SPARKLING

This should be self-explanatory. Wines come in either thick, heavy bottles with corks wrapped round with wire which are impossible to get out, in which case they are sparkling (i.e., fizzy, but for some reason this word must not be used of wines), or in ordinary bottles with ordinary corks which are impossible to get out, in which case they are still. The fun begins when you discover that many still wines are slightly fizzy, or rather, sparkling. Sometimes this is intentional, as with Portuguese Vinho Verde (literally 'green wine'). Even when it is not intentional, it's not necessarily considered a fault. The thing to do, in any case, is to say 'Hmm… slightly *pétillant*' (if it's French) or 'Possibly *spritzig*' (if it's German).

UNDERSTANDING THE LABEL

You will come across one additional obstacle in the path of appreciating wine: that of deciphering the sometimes arcane and confusing information that is printed on the label. The worst offenders here are undoubtedly the Germans, who compound the sin of overcomplicating their wine nomenclature with the use of unreadable Gothic type. If you can understand a German wine label, you can understand anything. French wine labels, on the other hand, are the leaders in sheer pretentiousness:

Grand Vin de Bordeaux Well, Bordeaux is a big area; the wine in question may not be all that grand.

Château La Tour de St-Hippolyte Some jumped-up little wine is trying to bask in reflected glory.

Appellation Bordeaux Supérieur Contrôlée Don't get too excited: the 'superior' just means it has a degree more alcohol.

Cuvée fûts neufs Oh no! It tastes like a DIY cabinet!

Millésime 1995 Don't take this too seriously. It's just a printed number.

Mis en Bouteille au Domaine Some guy with a mobile bottling line comes round to the backyard.

French Wine Made by Australians The Aussies are getting their own back.

If German wine labels contain too much information (and they do), others contain too little. Greek wines are particular offenders. Not only do they tend to be named after Greek gods (Aphrodite, Bacchus), tragic heroes (Othello, Orestes) or – mystifyingly – lavatory cleansers (Demestica), their labels tell you precisely nothing about the vintage, region or anything else you want to know. On the other hand, given the quality of some Greek wines, this may be a sensible policy...

In general, the things to look for on labels so as to hold forth in the appropriate direction consist of the following:

The vintage This item is usually clearly visible. Some wines are non-vintage, but of course you know that the only acceptable non-vintage wines are Sherry (which hardly ever has a vintage) and Champagne.

The grape variety Don't expect this in all cases. The aristocratic wines, such as Bordeaux and Burgundy, for instance, don't specify their grape varieties. You're expected to know them.

The country of origin Always look for this: some bottles carry the mark of shame, aka EU Tafelwein. This means they have been dredged up from the European Wine Lake and bottled by bureaucrats.

The region Look for initials like AC and DOC (and more recently, AOP and IGP), which tell you that the wine comes from a designated area. With Italian wines, though, this is mostly a bad thing.

Bottling information Whether the wine has been bottled at the château or estate (always considered a good thing), in the country of origin, or not (always considered a bad thing).

GREAT VINTAGES OF THE PAST

Vintages are like eighteenth-century battles. The French win most of them, the Germans put in the occasional brilliant victory, and the Italians don't try very hard.

It could be impressive, though probably completely useless, to be able to reel off a few of the great years of the past. Start with some of these below:

- The year of Halley's comet, 1811, and the year of Revolutions, 1848, are two easy ones to remember (probably easier to remember than to drink).

- Then, try 1870 – the clarets of that year took 80 years to come round – and the great pair of 1899 and 1900.

- Good vintages quite often come in pairs: 1928 and 1929, 1961 and 1962, 1970 and 1971, 1982 and 1983, 1985 and 1986, 1995 and 1996, 2000 and 2001, 2005 and 2006.

- On the other hand, good vintages also come singly: 1945, 1959, 1966, 1998, 2003. Or in trios: 1947, 1948 and 1949; 1988, 1989 and 1990; 2008, 2009 and 2010.

There are several things to note here:

1. When talking about great vintages, people always seem to mean great claret (otherwise known as Bordeaux) vintages.

2. Great claret vintages now occur, on average, about two years out of three.

3. So-called 'vintages of the century' occur at least twice a decade.

If someone says, 'Of course, 1928 was a wonderful vintage for claret,' you can try retorting, 'Yes, but very poor for Tokay,' or 'Yes, but a freak rainstorm practically destroyed the vintage in the Barossa Valley.' It's highly unlikely that the other person will know anything about old vintages in obscure areas.

A BIT OF HISTORY

The history of wine is very long and involved, stretching back as long as people have felt the need to pour a restorative glass after a long day's work. Mercifully, you need deal only with the last century or so, because the vines in Europe, Africa, and very nearly everywhere else were all but wiped out by a plague of aphids in the latter part of the nineteenth century.

This affliction, properly known as *Phylloxera vastatrix*, attacked and destroyed the roots of most grapevines. Fortunately it took nearly 30 years to do so. During that time – after trying various remedies which included the application of coffee grounds, incense and urine, and the burying of toads at the root – vine growers took the opportunity to import native vine rootstocks from the United States, which were partially resistant to the disease, and graft onto them what remained of the famous grape varieties.

Ironically, phylloxera is now destroying Californian vineyards, the Californians having subsequently (and unfortunately) planted some European grape varieties on less-than-totally-phylloxera-resistant rootstocks.

ESSENTIAL EQUIPMENT

Unlike some other art forms, wine has to be bought and consumed in order to be appreciated, so some type of initial investment is required. There are also a few bits of fairly vital equipment with which bluffers should familiarise themselves.

A NOSE

90% of the 'taste' of wine is perceived via the olfactory bulb above your nostrils. The taste buds on your tongue can detect only five basic sensations – sweet, bitter, salty, sour and 'umami' (useful for Japanese food) – which is why your sense of taste is always impaired by a blocked nose. The prose tumbling forth from the mouths of wine critics comes from a higher plane.

The most legendary nose in the wine business was owned by the late Don José Ignacio Domecq, aka *El Nariz* ('The Nose'), of the eponymous Sherry firm. His knowledgeable nose was long and beaky, able to penetrate the small, tapered Sherry glasses called *copitas* like the proboscis of a hummingbird. It is probably a case of natural selection, given that the business was in his family for generations. Non-Sherry tasters do not need such an impressive hooter, but the equipment inside it must be operative.

CORKSCREW

Wine comes in bottles with corks for which, unfortunately, no really satisfactory device for extraction has yet been invented. One can understand why, in the old days, choleric gentlemen used to decapitate bottles with red-hot pincers, but this is sadly out of fashion, and in any case difficult without a blazing fire. You should probably opt for a simple 'waiter's friend', with its unfolding, pocket-knife-inspired design. At the other extreme is the Screwpull Lever Corkscrew, which, at the price of a plane ticket from London to Bordeaux, is only for the serious, but enables even the feeblest to extract the most stubborn cork without perspiring.

Types of corkscrew to be avoided include the bulbous 'Russian doll' variety – you can't see what you're doing with it and the handle tends to come off mid-screw; the double-armed ratchet type, which has a drill-like action that can bore a hole through the cork and can catch your fingers in its ratchets; or the vacuum variety that pumps the air out – this can blow up the bottle. Go for the simplest kind so long as it has a good wire worm screw and a comfortable, firmly attached handle.

Bottles sealed with untwistable screwcaps render corkscrews obsolete – and old fogeys apoplectic. This is silly on two counts because screwcaps remove any chance of a wine being 'corked', or infected by tainted corks, and can be opened quickly in case of emergency. Only the finest wines intended for lengthy ageing – i.e., nothing you would buy in a supermarket – might require a traditional cork. It is thought that the trace amounts of oxygen that pass through a cork *might* help with the ageing process, but the jury is still out on this one. Conversely, an airtight screwcapped wine cannot be 'screwed'.

It is generally agreed that wine should be drunk from a glass, although for the desperate, any watertight receptacle will do.

Plastic corks, in contrast, are the work of the Devil, requiring biceps of steel to remove – or gelignite as a last resort.

A GLASS

It is generally agreed that wine should be drunk from a glass, although for the desperate, any watertight receptacle will do. Glasses have the advantage of not affecting the flavour in the way that leather bottles, metal goblets and dancing slippers can. You can also see what you're drinking. The kind of glass is relatively unimportant, although a tulip shape, which gathers the bouquet, guiding it towards your nose (*see* 'Smell', page 30) is considered best for most wines. Otherwise, the simpler the better – it's easier to wash up.

Bluffers should at least be aware, however, of expensive Riedel glassware from Austria, whose natural habitat is in restaurants with starched linen and *sommeliers* (wine waiters to you and me). Basically, Riedel has created a range of more than 250 glasses, each designed to wring maximum pleasure from specific grape varieties and regions. A Riedel Chardonnay glass, for example, is shaped only for Chardonnay, to show off this wine's aromas to best effect, and guide the wine to the most Chardonnay-friendly part of the tongue. You should also know that squillions of Riedel glasses have been sold. As a bluffer, you could insist on these glasses when dining out, describing them (in the company's own words) as 'precision instruments to convey the message of the wine'. Secretly, you might regard them as tasting tools – for tools.

A DECANTER

Many wine buffs believe that allowing a wine to 'breathe' before serving it is a good idea. This is based on the notion that exposing wine to oxygen helps it to 'open up' and release its bouquet. Simply removing the cork to allow a wine to breathe is useless because the surface area exposed to the air is so small. The best way to let it breathe properly is to pour some into a glass when you open the bottle. This not only increases the surface area exposed to oxygen, but enables you to snaffle a sneaky glass ahead of the game.

Alternatively, you could aerate your wine by pouring it into a decanter, but expect this to cause all sorts of ructions if a wine bore is present. According to the late Professor Émile Peynaud, one of the most revered oenologists in the history of Bordeaux, there is no valid reason for decanting a wine other than to remove any sediment that might be lurking at the bottom of the bottle. Thus, he believed it was pointless to decant anything other than venerable old red wines or vintage and crusted Port. Peynaud even argued that decanting old wines actually serves to diffuse the bouquet, causing them to fade rapidly. Decanting old wines, therefore, is a risky business: less so for everyday plonk.

Decanting is easy, but it must be made to look as difficult as possible.

Decanting is the process of pouring the contents into a decanter and stopping before the gunge gets in. It sounds easy. It *is* easy. But it must be made to look as difficult as possible. The aim is to make the performance resemble a Black Mass. A candle should be brought into use, supposedly so that you can see when the sediment reaches the neck, but rather more to induce a ceremonial atmosphere. Absolute silence must be observed and a look of rapt concentration maintained until the last drop of clear liquid has been transferred.

After this, a dramatic sigh, a wipe of the brow and momentary indication of emotional exhaustion, as of an actor having just played a great tragic role, may be called for to underline the risk involved. It is particularly important to sniff the cork of the bottle being decanted: it may then be attached to the neck of the decanter. This is roughly equivalent to handing back to the patient an organ that has been surgically removed.

The decanting of white wines has usually been considered unnecessary. Besides, the visual effect could be unpleasantly medical (which is perhaps why white wine is usually put in green bottles). Nevertheless, an effective gambit is to insist on the decanting of fine white Burgundy, especially Meursault and *grand cru* Chablis. For the unscrupulous, this is also a way of passing off your heavily oaked and inexpensive white Rioja or Chardonnay as something more classy. And by all means decant an inexpensive Port if you want to pass it off as vintage.

CELLAR AND STORAGE

Bluffers should not be afraid to talk about their 'cellar', even if they don't possess anything remotely approximating an underground room. A 'cellar' for these purposes is a collection of at least two bottles, or possibly a single bottle of reasonable quality. If you're keeping wine for any length of time, however, there are two important rules to observe:

1. To keep corks from drying out and letting air in, bottles should be kept lying down or, better still,

upside down. This will look suitably eccentric, but it is in fact a relatively common way of transporting or storing wine.

2. Wine should be kept somewhere with a reasonably constant temperature, preferably not above 15.5°C: roughly like a fairly cool day. This is likely to be impossible to achieve, however, in which case it's best to remember that a constant temperature of 21°C is better than a fluctuation between 4.5°C and 15.5°C. The other solution, of course, is simply to drink your wine quickly before it has a chance to go off.

Poor cellaring conditions do have one advantage, however: wine will mature more quickly in them. For example, certain Bordeaux vintages that have taken ages to come around (1970, 1975) might be greatly improved by a spell in a centrally heated flat.

TEMPERATURE CONTROL

After aroma, taste and texture, temperature is the fourth dimension of wine, and it exerts a huge influence on the whole sensory package. Served too cold, white wines lose much of their aroma and flavour – which is no bad thing with a bottle of 'paint stripper' but a tragic waste of anything rich and complex, like a fine white Burgundy. Describe a red wine that is served too warm as 'flabby' and 'unfocused', and complain that the alcohol dominates. Argue that the cruel practice of pre-warming reds on Agas and radiators lends new meaning to the term 'cooking wine' and should be banned along with seal clubbing. The accepted rule these days is that most red wines should be served at room temperature (the French term is *chambré*) and most white wines lightly chilled – that is to say, having spent an hour in the fridge or 12 minutes in the freezer.

Wine snobs tend to be suspicious of the freezer, which really suggests that they once forgot to remove a bottle before it exploded or the contents turned into a Slush Puppie. If, however, you're absolutely gagging for a thoroughly chilled glass of white, and your bottle is stubbornly warm, a wizard wheeze is to pour a glass into a resealable freezer bag and stick it in the freezer for a short spell.

The general consensus is that the optimum temperature for big, spicy reds like Aussie Shiraz, red Rhône and Zinfandel is about 18°C. Medium-bodied reds like Rioja and Chianti are better slightly cooler at around 16°C. Fuller-bodied, complex whites like the above-mentioned Burgundy or rich, oaky New World Chardonnays project well at around 12–14°C. Medium- to lighter-bodied whites such as Chablis and Sauvignon Blanc are good at about 9 or 10°C, as is a crisp rosé. Err on the cool side when serving, as a glass of wine warms quickly in your cupped hands: *chaleur de la main*, as the French call it.

It's terribly fashionable to chill certain red wines these days, and the bluffer needs to be *au fait* with the styles where this is socially acceptable. These include lighter-bodied, unoaked, juicy reds like Beaujolais (made from the Gamay grape), Loire reds (Cabernet

Franc), and lighter-bodied Pinot Noir, Barbera and Valpolicella. A light chill seems to exaggerate both their smooth texture and crisp acidity.

You should also chill dry fino Sherry, tawny Port and sweet wines like Sauternes and Muscat de Beaumes-de-Venise to show that you seem to know what you are doing.

There is, of course, an intermediate state between chilled and *chambré*, namely cellar temperature. This is a very useful category because it can mean the temperature the wine happens to be when you have forgotten to chill or warm it.

Tasting *is a professional activity which people do to earn a living. It is done standing up, and involves rude noises, wry faces and spittoons.*
Drinking, *on the other hand, is a pleasure. It is done sitting down, except at drinks parties, which in any case are seldom a pleasure.*

TASTING AND DRINKING

Bluffers should never forget that tasting and drinking are two distinct activities and should never be confused. *Tasting* is a professional activity which people do to earn a living. It is done standing up, and involves rude noises, wry faces and spittoons. Tasters never swallow. (Well, hardly ever…) One man at a smart London tasting was heard asking another, 'What do you think of the Niederhäuser Hermannshöhle Spätlese 1985?' The other paused judiciously before replying, 'I honestly don't know, but it slips down a treat.'

Drinking, on the other hand, is a pleasure. It is done sitting down, except at drinks parties, which in any case are seldom a pleasure. It is true that if you are drinking decent wine you should go through some of the motions of tasting, but you will do so in a different spirit.

The motions of tasting are outlined below:

1. Pour out a little wine, filling the glass no more than a quarter full. Stare fixedly at it. Look mean. If it's red, tilt the glass and hold it against a white surface.

Viewing the meniscus (where the surface of the liquid meets the glass) against a white background shows the wine's true colour clearly. It also provides a perfect excuse to hold your glass against other, more interesting white surfaces such as a white blouse or shirt front. It's a fact that only one wine shows a greenish tinge at the meniscus: Sherry. But it is probably easier to rely on the fact that it says 'Sherry' on the bottle…

2. Hold the glass firmly by the base and swirl it around either clockwise or anticlockwise (but not both at the same time). Swirling requires a little practice: too vigorous a swirl will send the wine sloshing over the edge; too little vigour will have no effect on it whatsoever. The theory is that it releases the bouquet. In fact, it proves you're a pro.

3. Having swirled, you're ready to sniff. Here, an impressively shaped nose undoubtedly helps. Blocked sinuses do not. Some people favour moving the nose from side to side over the wine, presumably to give each nostril its share, but this can look rather sinister.

4. Only after these preliminaries is it permissible to take liquid into your mouth. A fairly large sip in contrast to the measure in the glass is the thing, but not too large that it prevents you from performing the most difficult trick, which is to take in a small amount of air with an audible sucking noise at the same time as the wine. This is supposed to aerate the wine in your

mouth and release more flavour. It is not the same as gargling. You should try to avoid gargling – unless you have a sore throat. Wine, after all, is an antiseptic.

5. Having swilled it about a bit, spit out the wine as elegantly as possible into a spittoon, box of sawdust or potted plant. There is a marked spitting order at some tastings. Watch out for this or you will get indelible young claret upon your front. Mind you, it's easy to put it there yourself.

6. Surreptitiously drink some of the wine that you liked the best.

7. Take notes on all stages except (6).

When drinking a good wine, or one that your host considers good, limit yourself to tilting, swirling and sniffing before drinking. Do these things in a gracious, smiling manner, rather than with the fixed, suspicious glare of the professional taster. Do not try to take in air with the wine. You may not be asked back again.

A drinker should not fill his glass more than half-full if he is going to attempt swirling. He may feel that this is too great a sacrifice.

WINE-SPEAK

For some reason, many people feel that drinking – or even tasting and drinking – wine is not enough; they must also talk about it. Indeed, conversation about wine occupies most of the time at social gatherings among the wine-loving fraternity. You may secretly find this boring or pretentious, but as a bluffer you need to be able not only to drink and taste wine properly but also to hold your own in wine-speak.

A wine deemed overly alcoholic is described as 'hot' which, uniquely in wine circles, is not a compliment.

This is a complicated subject, but these few simple rules can get you a surprisingly long way:

1. Try never to use words except where they are strictly necessary. Noises that are either non-committal (such as 'Hmm....') or enthusiastic ('Mmm....', 'Ahh!') and interesting facial contortions (raised eyebrows, narrowed glance, pursed lips) are often entirely adequate, and don't actually commit you to anything.

2. The word 'Yes' is quite sufficient in most cases – not least because it can be said in an almost infinite variety of tones: doubtful, quizzical, interrogative, tentative, affirmative, decisive, appreciative, ecstatic. It can be repeated in a clipped, conversation-stopping manner ('Yes, yes.'), or in a rising, excited tone ('Yes, yes, YES!').

3. Put off describing what the wine actually tastes like for as long as possible. Instead, limit yourself to some of the following technical expressions.

   a) Mention ullage. This means the level of wine in the bottle. If you've noticed that the bottle is not completely full, say in a neutral tone: 'Ah, slightly ullaged.' It could be, of course, that your host has swigged some of it beforehand.

   b) Ask whether the wine has 'thrown a deposit'. Deposit, of course, refers to sediment at the bottom of the bottle, not what you get back when you return empties to the off-licence.

   c) If you've noticed when you're tilting the wine that it leaves a thick, transparent trail on the glass (as most red wines do), say that it has 'good legs'. Thicker, viscous 'legs' are an indication of higher alcohol. A wine deemed overly alcoholic is described as 'hot' which, uniquely in wine circles, is not a compliment.

APPEARANCE

Once you've exhausted these gambits, talk about the colour. You're on fairly safe ground here unless you are colour-blind, since it is easier to describe visual phenomena rather than tastes or smells. It might be a good idea to brush up on your metals and semi-precious stones: different shades of gold, amber, garnet, ruby, etc., seem to go down particularly well.

SMELL

When talking about smell, do not use the word 'smell'. In English, this usually has unpleasant connotations. Instead, choose from 'nose' (which with wine doesn't have unpleasant associations), 'aroma', or 'bouquet', if you're feeling flowery.

If the wine doesn't smell of anything, try: 'Rather dumb on the nose, don't you find?' or 'It's still very closed.' Alternatively, if it smells very strongly, you can say, 'It's very forward on the nose.' None of these comments, of course, commits you to an opinion of the wine's quality. If you have to be more specific, choose from some of the more commonly used 'nose' words, below:

Oaky, buttery, vanilla-ey All of these are used interchangeably to describe certain wines that spend time in oak barrels, especially red Rioja, white Burgundy and the latter wine's Californian and Australian clones.

Blackcurrant Only use this word when you have checked that the wine is made from the Cabernet Sauvignon grape.

Spicy Especially useful for describing Syrah/Shiraz, Zinfandel or Gewürztraminer. This is a very vague term considering how many different spices there are, but such things do not worry the cognoscenti.

Of course, people will say that wines smell of anything: violets, truffles (both the kind pigs dig up in Périgord and the delicious, dusted chocolate balls), beetroot, sweaty saddles, wet socks, farmyards, petrol (used of old Rieslings, which can have a curious oily whiff, and best said, like so many things, in French: *goût de pétrole*). The noble Pinot Noir, from which red Burgundy is fashioned, is particularly prone to the odour of excrement. In fact, one wine writer said of a Burgundy, with the air of one bestowing a compliment, 'Bags of poo!'

Smells are clearly oddly evocative, and yet often these correspondences seem entirely personal and don't work for others. There's nothing to stop you from trying this kind of thing, and the more personal the better, because it cannot then be disproved. For instance: 'This wine reminds me of an evening I spent in Crete. I don't know exactly what the connection is – the wild thyme, the sea air, the herd of goats in the distance…'

DESCRIBING WINE

It is a truth universally acknowledged that there are too few words to describe tastes: 'sweet', 'dry', 'acidic' are simply not enough. There isn't even a generally agreed word for the opposite of acidic, and it's doubtful whether there are other definitive words to describe the taste of wine, since few wines are either salty or bitter enough for those two other unmistakable qualities to come into play. All the rest is metaphor: a poet's dream, but a bluffer's nightmare. Before you despair, know that you can get quite a lot of mileage out of the three main terms: sweetness, dryness and acidity.

SWEETNESS AND DRYNESS

Degrees of sweetness and dryness are perhaps on the obvious side, but in wine-speak there's no harm in stating the obvious. It is particularly useful if you know how sweet or how dry a wine is meant to be, and then can suggest that it somehow contradicts expectations. Thus, 'Surprisingly dry for a Sauternes/Beerenauslese' or 'This Chablis isn't as bone-dry as I would have expected' are effective because they show others that:

a) you know your stuff; and

b) you have original, even if wrong, opinions.

Almost all red wines, incidentally, are dry. There isn't much point in saying that a claret (Bordeaux) is dry; opine that your host's Château Lafite is surprisingly sweet and you may not be given a second glass.

ACIDITY

You can get a lot further by talking about acidity. Acidity in wine, funnily enough, is generally considered a good thing, and so the comment 'Good acidity' can work wonders. This is especially true of white wines, in which acidity is synonymous with freshness. A white wine with too little acidity can be criticised for being 'heavy', 'flat' or simply 'fat' (*see* 'Body', page 35).

Wines can, of course, sometimes be too acidic. This especially tends to be a fault of wines from cold countries and regions such as Germany, Champagne and England. Comments on excess acidity are often expressed in involuntary, physical forms.

Without getting too technical, wine contains different kinds of acidity. The best, tartaric and lactic for instance, don't have a pronounced taste but do impart freshness or zinginess to the wine. Other kinds of acidity do have a marked taste: malic acid, for instance, makes wine taste like apples, which is not necessarily a bad thing. 'Appley' is a good word to use to describe Mosel wines, for instance.

The worst kind of acidity is acetic, also known as vinegar. If you think a wine tastes vinegary but don't want to upset your host, say, 'This wine has rather high volatile acidity, don't you think?' Put this way, it isn't considered nearly so rude.

BALANCE

Yet even good acidity on its own is not enough; a wine needs to be balanced. Balance is perhaps the key concept in the wine world. Fortunately nobody ever asks exactly what is balanced with what; the idea is that all the constituent parts of a wine – alcohol, acidity, fruit – are roughly in harmony.

Unlike unbalanced people, unbalanced wines don't do unpredictable things: in fact, they are usually very ordinary. A perfectly balanced wine is actually a rare and wonderful creature.

TANNIN

Here is a more friendly term for the bluffer. Tannin is a preservative substance extracted from the grape skins, pips and stems, found mainly in red wine. It is easily recognisable because it grips the back of your teeth – rather like those little sucker things the dentist puts in your mouth. Also like the dentist, tannin leaves your teeth in need of the services of a hygienist. Young red wines that are the opposite of mellow are likely to be tannic.

'Hard' and 'tannic' are two adjectives that commonly go together, particularly when you're tasting young claret, one of the most unpleasant of all aesthetic experiences. If you're given a claret and find it about as attractive and yielding as a Scottish bank manager, you may say, 'Still rather tannic, I find.'

There is a danger here. Some wines, especially clarets – like some bank managers no doubt – pass from being unpleasantly hard and tannic (that is to say, too young) to being unpleasantly 'dried out' (too old) without any intervening stage of pleasant mellowness.

FRUIT

This might seem the most obvious quality of a wine's taste, but fruit is the starting point of wine: the substance from which it's made. Thus, to say that a wine is 'fruity' is to suggest that it has gone through all the processes which have transformed it from uninteresting grapes into a miraculous drink for nothing.

'Fruity' should be your last resort. 'Grapey' is a somewhat different matter, because only wines made from certain kinds of grapes, especially Muscat, actually taste, or should taste, of grapes.

BODY

This is an essential description. Unlike post-Renoir women, wines generally aspire to be full-bodied. Wines with insufficient body are said to be 'thin', which isn't a compliment. On the other hand, wines with too much body can be called 'fat', which is slightly insulting.

Male wine people, particularly after a glass or two, are especially prone to talk about wine in female terms (the Germans are the main culprits). For example: 'This is the beautiful girl you take to the opera… and this is the woman you marry.'

GENERAL TASTING NOTES

There are, of course, all kinds of other approaches to talking about the taste of wine. There is some famous advice to be 'boldly meaningless' and talk about 'cornery wines' and other such things. You can always try long German words. Then there is the *Brideshead Revisited* style: abominably precious (for instance, 'shy, like a gazelle', or 'a fullish body but it's beginning to fade') but possibly due for resuscitation.

At the other extreme there is the blunt Antipodean approach that's mainly prevalent Down Under, such as: 'Not a wine to wrap around your tonsils.'

One all-embracing term you can offer is 'pronounced'. The bluffer can get a lot of mileage from this one. For instance: 'This wine has a pronounced bouquet, don't you think?' is a completely safe comment that still manages to sound informed.

If an appropriate opinion escapes you but you find that you're nonetheless obliged to give one, then it makes good sense to be as non-specific as possible, as in: 'Hmm. This is coarse, but generous.'

Here are some other plausible comments that could leave your audience satisfied, if none the wiser:

'Somewhat lacking in finesse.'

'Broad and weighty.'

'Voluptuous, but in an earthy way.'

'Interesting depth.'

'Ripe, but lacking concentration.'

'Concentrated, but lacking ripeness.'

'Over-ripe, but with a touch of tartness.'

'Elegant, but lacks backbone.'

GRAPE VARIETIES

By now you know that wine is made from fermented grape juice, and you also know (as if you need to be reminded) that only wine made from the Muscat variety actually tastes of grapes. The rest taste 'winey', but you'll have to do better than that if you want to give the impression that you know what you're talking about.

Frustratingly, there is a long tradition of labelling wines geographically (i.e., comes from Bordeaux or Rioja), which adds to the mystique but is less than helpful. Recently though, thanks to the more prosaic New World winemakers, many wines are labelled according to grape variety. This at least gives you a fighting chance of correctly identifying what grape has been used. Ampelographers (vine boffins) can reel off hundreds of grape varieties, but the grapes mentioned here should be ample for bluffing purposes.

Although there are just two major grape families, *Vitis vinifera* and *Vitis labrusca* (the former producing the great majority of the world's wines), there are more than 5,000 different wine grape varieties. Happily, you don't need to know all of them.

RED GRAPES

CABERNET SAUVIGNON

The most famous red Bordeaux grape, now also grown in California, Australia, Spain, Italy, Bulgaria, Chile, Moldova, etc. It has in fact become the world's number-one red-wine grape. This could be because wines made from it taste rather like Ribena. They also taste roughly the same wherever the grape is grown, which is useful because you know what you'll get.

Tasting note Unmistakable blackcurrant character (call this 'cassis' if you want to sound pretentious, or French). Other notes include green pepper, asparagus, cedar and incense. State confidently that it can be 'tough and tannic when young'.

Gamay smells of boiled sweets, bananas and bubblegum. It is thus popular with drinkers wanting to get in touch with their inner child.

GAMAY

The purple grape that puts the 'jolly' into Beaujolais. You might remember this quip the next time it is served at a dinner party. Or maybe not. Gamay's soft aromas and lightness of touch are often boosted by something called 'carbonic maceration', in which whole bunches of grapes are sealed, uncrushed, in vats filled with carbon dioxide where each berry undergoes a swift internal fermentation. This technique, favoured for light-bodied, fruity reds for drinking young, produces aromas of boiled sweets, bananas and bubblegum. It is thus popular with drinkers wanting to get in touch with their inner child. Gamay is also grown in the cool, northerly Loire Valley, where winemakers greatly appreciate its ability to ripen early.

Tasting note Simple raspberry and strawberry aromas, with a floral touch of roses and violets and occasional hints, not surprisingly, of Bazooka Joe. Served lightly chilled, Gamay's sprightly acidity is a perfect foil for *charcuterie*.

GRENACHE

Originally from northern Spain, where bluffers should point out that it is called Garnacha, this grape variety crossed the Pyrenees into southern France, where it adopted its 'international' name of Grenache. In Spain, it's pretty big in Navarra, Penedès, Priorato, Somontano and Rioja, where it helps to soften Tempranillo (*see* page 42). In France, Grenache is widespread in Languedoc-Roussillon, Provence and the southern Rhône. It's also the leading player in Châteauneuf-du-Pape's 13 approved grape varieties – one of which, weirdly, is white – and is the blushing hero of many French rosés, especially Tavel and Lirac.

Tasting note Red fruit like strawberries and raspberries when young, turning darker (blackcurrants, blackberries, black cherries, even black olives) with age and limited yields. Can be 'quite leathery and spicy'.

MALBEC

Malbec was a minor player in Bordeaux blends until it was wiped out in 'the great frost of 1956' (you're probably too young to remember), but with Gallic ennui they couldn't be bothered to replant it. More recently, Argentina has adopted Malbec as its signature red grape and transformed it into a star. It's still the major component in 'the black wine' of Cahors, as it's described by English merchants, and is blended with Gamay and Cabernet Franc in the Loire.

Tasting note Big and beefy, with dark, damson fruit and violet aromas. Luscious, gamey and perfect with Argentinian beef – which must be poetic justice.

MERLOT

The other red grape of Bordeaux, also grown in California, Italy, Bulgaria, Chile and everywhere else. It often makes more palatable wines than Cabernet Sauvignon (less tough and tannic), but is deemed not as good, possibly because wines made from it don't taste of Ribena. Its laid-back style makes it especially popular in California.

Tasting note Few winemakers seem to agree on what Merlot should taste of. The spectrum usually ranges from strawberries to leather, depending on the age. Fruit-cake flavours sometimes pop up in Bordeaux samples. In most cases, it's soft.

PINOT NOIR

Here is a red grape with a notoriously temperamental and difficult character. An artistic type which, like Solzhenitsyn, Ovid and Oscar Wilde, goes into a decline when exiled – in this case, from its native lands of Burgundy and Champagne. You can enthuse about Hamilton Russell's faux Côtes de Nuits from Hermanus, South Africa. And the editor of these guides insists that Tasmania produces an estimable Pinot Noir, especially from the Bay of Fires winery.

Tasting note Elusive but unmistakable – can be anything from wild strawberry to beetroot, white truffle, decaying vegetables and even excrement (but in a good way).

SANGIOVESE

Sangiovese is the archetypal Tuscan grape and mainstay of Chianti. Given the quality of most Chianti until recently, Tuscans used to keep quiet about Sangiovese and dilute it with Trebbiano (which at least tasted neutral), or else call it by other names when they wanted it to sound classy (Brunello di Montalcino). Now Sangiovese is suddenly sexy and being cultivated all over the place, especially in Argentina and California (where there are loads of Italians) and even Texas (where there are fewer).

Tasting note Sweet-sour cherries, savoury sun-dried tomatoes and, sometimes, a whiff of violets.

SYRAH

Well-liked by the Aussies, but they call it 'Shiraz' – not to be confused with the wine produced in the Iranian city of the same name; that's called Shirazi. Possibly the world's most undervalued red grape, Syrah is used to make the great northern Rhône wines.

Tasting note Spicy, with wild berries, wild herbs or pretty much anything that's wild and hirsute (though not mountain goat).

TEMPRANILLO

Tempranillo is the Spanish equivalent of Sangiovese, and this grape is used not just for Rioja but for nearly every Spanish red wine you've ever heard of, and some you may not have. The name means 'little early ripener', and the taste could be said to be not very interesting without the addition of lashings of oak – which is why Rioja traditionally spends years in oak barrels and Rioja lookalikes have clumps of oak chips suspended in them like tea bags. Tempranillo is also being grown in Argentina and California (where they'll usually try anything).

Tasting note Fruit notes range from wild strawberry to stewed plum. Has strong vanilla overtones and the smell of a furniture warehouse from the oak treatment.

ZINFANDEL

A Californian grape with a notoriously split personality and obscure origins, Zinfandel can be used to make sweet, jammy, jug wine or the tellingly named 'blush' Zinfandel, an insipid pale rosé which ought to induce a blush in its makers. In the right hands, however, especially those of Paul Draper of Ridge Vineyards, it can be transformed into a rich, concentrated, blood-red nectar. Its origins are not really obscure at all: it's the same as the southern Italian Primitivo, but presumably Californians didn't like the sound of that.

Tasting note A full spice rack of flavours, including black pepper, clove and cinnamon. Berry fruits come to the fore, though in the case of blush 'Zin', they taste more like talcum powder.

WHITE GRAPES

ALBARIÑO

In green Galicia, northern Spain, Albariño makes the most fashionable and expensive Spanish white wines, notably in the subregion of Rías Baixas. Across the border in northern Portugal, it's called Alvarinho and makes the best Vinho Verde (other, lesser grapes are permitted).

Tasting note Aromatic stone fruit (peaches and apricots) with a squeeze of citrus (lemon and lime) and a good blast of acidity.

CHARDONNAY

The grape that is used to make white Burgundy and Champagne (the latter, though, along with two red varieties, Pinot Noir and Pinot Meunier). It, too, is grown successfully in California, Australia, Spain, Italy, Bulgaria, Chile, etc., and is now the world's number-one white grape. Anyone aspiring to originality of palate, like yourself, must greet its appearance with a weary sigh or, better still, the counter-suggestion of an obscure southern French Viognier, an Austrian Grüner Veltliner or a Galician Albariño.

Tasting note Confusing variety of possibilities from stones (Chablis) and unspecified flowers (just use the adjective 'floral') through to butter, double cream and even hazelnuts in mature white Burgundy. Australia pioneered the rich and popular tropical, pineapple-chunk style with lashings of new oak.

CHENIN BLANC

A schizophrenic grape, making so-so, crisp, fresh whites in South Africa, but some of the world's best dry and sweet wines in favoured corners of its native Loire. In the middle Loire region, home of Anjou, Saumur and Touraine, Chenin Blanc is quite possibly the world's most versatile grape, making most styles of white wine – still and sparkling, dry and sweet – in every permutation. In Australia, its notably high acidity breathes life into Chardonnay and Semillon blends.

Tasting note Where do you start? Honey, orange blossom and damp straw are frequently used descriptors.

GEWÜRZTRAMINER

Also known as Traminer, but that was apparently too short and easy to pronounce. This grape, mainly grown in Alsace (where it drops the Germanic umlaut), imparts a pronounced, spicy aroma and rich flavour, a character that has been colourfully compared to the odour of a South American brothel. You either love it or hate it.

Tasting note Lychees, Turkish delight, rose water and any other scent associated with a Paraguayan house of ill repute.

MUSCAT

At last, the one that makes wines that taste of grapes. Muscat is the oldest-known grape variety, dating back to Greek and Roman antiquity. There are numerous branches of the Muscat family, including Muscat of Alexandria, Muscat Blanc à Petits Grains and Muscat Ottonel, some of which are pink-skinned. This family is as talented and versatile as the Osmonds, making an enormous variety of wines, ranging from the deep-brown Liqueur Muscats of Australia to the golden dessert wines of Muscat de Frontignan and Beaumes-de-Venise, and frothy fizz like Moscato d'Asti. The French describe it as *musqué* ('musky').

The Muscat family is as talented and versatile as the Osmonds, making an enormous variety of wines.

Tasting note Depends on the style, but generally strongly perfumed: jasmine, honeysuckle, orange blossom, rose petals and elderflower with a touch of citrus. Oh, yes: and grapes. As a contrast, Australian Liqueur Muscats taste of coffee and toffee.

PINOT GRIS/GRIGIO

Possibly the most remarkable thing about this grape, and the best source of bluffing potential, is the sheer number of names it goes under: Pinot Gris or Tokay in France, Pinot Grigio in Italy, Ruländer or Grauburgunder in Germany. Probably best from Alsace, Oregon and New Zealand.

Tasting note If Italian, generally lacking in discernible flavour; late-harvested examples from Alsace can show a musky aroma, and gingery spiciness.

RIESLING

The most important thing is to pronounce this grape's name properly: it's *Ree-zling*, not *Rye-zling*. The next most important thing is to be aware that a lot of so-called Riesling, e.g., Welschriesling, grown confusingly in Slovakia, and the Lutomer Riesling, is not real Riesling at all. The true Riesling is the best German grape and makes rather tart wines which you may correctly call 'steely'. When they get older, you call them 'petrolly' – after the little-known variant called Diesling, which can be used to fuel taxis.

Tasting note Green apple and white peach when young, honey and petrol when old.

SAUVIGNON BLANC

Fashionable white grape variety, it is pretty tart and supposed to impart the smell of crushed nettles. This is the grape that is used to make Sancerre and Pouilly-Fumé, which is why in California (where they grow it, and everything else) it is called Fumé Blanc.

Tasting note Gooseberry and nettle when grown in the Loire or New Zealand (where it can acquire a whiff of tomcat); tropical passion fruit and pineapple when it's grown in California or Australia.

SÉMILLON/SEMILLON

Possibly the world's most undervalued white grape. The 'noble rot' botrytis (*see* Glossary, page 149) likes to attack it, especially in Sauternes. The Australians are going for Sémillon in a big way, and the grape seems to thrive on the rot. Sémillon (which loses its acute accent outside of France) is often used as a 'bulking' wine: get a fairly decent but smallish yield from various vineyards and bulk up the quantity with Sémillon, then sell it as a blend, like Sémillon/Chardonnay.

Tasting note This one is difficult to describe –'neutral' is the polite term – unless it has been attacked by noble rot or staves of new oak. Although it's fresh and citric when young, Sémillon can show hints of honey on toast with age (and oak).

TORRONTÉS

Argentina's unique white grape, thought to be a natural cross between Criolla Chica, planted by Jesuit missionaries, and Muscat of Alexandria. It ripens to perfection in the arid, high-altitude conditions of the Andes, where it can reach a deceptively high 14% alcohol by volume (abv).

Tasting note Floral aromas of jasmine and orange blossom with a dash of peach and passion fruit and a crisp, citrusy palate.

VIOGNIER

Once obscure and used only in the tiny Rhône appellations of Condrieu and Château-Grillet, this white grape variety is now appearing all over the place, from South Australia to Santa Cruz, California, and is being hailed in some quarters as the new Chardonnay. The bluffer can cast doubt on these claims, especially in relation to the inexpensive supermarket Viogniers from southern France (suggest that the 'yields are much too high').

Tasting note Luscious peach and nectarine on the nose, but the key quality is a rich, oily texture, or 'mouth-feel'.

GRAPE VARIETY BLENDS

A good bluffing line is that single varieties are old hat and dull. Point out that traditional red Bordeaux is a blend of Cabernet Sauvignon, Merlot, Cabernet Franc and Petit Verdot. Châteauneuf-du-Pape is made from as many as 13 grape varieties, principally Grenache, Mourvèdre, Cinsault and Syrah. Enthuse about blends such as Tempranillo/Cabernet Sauvignon (used to great effect in Navarra), Sangiovese/Cabernet Sauvignon (pioneered by Antinori with Tignanello), Shiraz/Cabernet Sauvignon, Syrah/Viognier and Roussanne/Viognier.

Commit these to memory, otherwise you might end up with a Zinfandel/Traminer (which could be a form of public transport in Eastern Europe).

Grape	Wine	Makes	Blended with	Grown
ALBARIÑO	White	Varietals; some blends. Rías Baixas, Vinho Verde	Loureiro, Treixadura	Spain, Portugal (as Alvarinho)
CABERNET SAUVIGNON	Red, rosé	Varietals; red Bordeaux; other blends such as Navarra (with Tempranillo), Tignanello (with Sangiovese)	Cabernet Franc, Cinsault, Malbec, Merlot, Petit Verdot; also Sangiovese, Syrah/Shiraz, Tempranillo	Worldwide
CHARDONNAY	White, sparkling	Varietals; Chablis and other white Burgundy, Champagne	Chenin Blanc, Colombard, Sémillon	Worldwide
CHENIN BLANC	White, sparkling	Varietals; Anjou, Touraine, Vouvray	Chardonnay, Sémillon	Australia, France (Loire), South Africa
GAMAY	Red, rosé; also sparkling (rare)	Varietals, blends. Beaujolais (crus, Villages, Nouveau); Coteaux d'Ancenis, Loire reds	Malbec	France (Loire Valley); also Switzerland and Eastern Europe
GEWÜRZTRAMINER	White, dry, sweet, fortified, sparkling	Mainly varietals: Vendange Tardive and Sélection de Grains Nobles. Some blends	Chardonnay, Muscat, Riesling	France (Alsace), Italy, Germany, New Zealand, Australia, California, Oregon, Chile
GRENACHE (NOIR)/ GARNACHA	Red, rosé, sweet, fortified	Mainly blends: Châteauneuf-du-Pape, Priorat, Rioja. Also rosés: Lirac, Tavel; dessert wines: Banyuls; fortifieds: vin doux naturel	Cabernet Sauvignon, Carignan, Cinsault, Mourvédre, Syrah; also Cariñena, Tempranillo…	France (Languedoc-Roussillon, Provence, southern Rhône); Spain (Navarra, Penedès, Priorato, Rioja, Somontano); Australia
MALBEC	Red	Varietals; also blends: Cahors	Gamay, Cabernet Franc, Merlot, Tannat	Mainly Argentina, France
MERLOT	Red	Varietals; blends: red Bordeaux	Cabernet Sauvignon	Worldwide, very popular in California
MUSCAT	White, sweet, sparkling, fortified	Dessert wines: Liqueur Muscat, Muscat de Rivesaltes, de Frontignan, Beaumes-de-Venise; sparkling: Moscato d'Asti; also dry table wine in France (Alsace); vin doux naturel	Gewürztraminer, Viognier	Europe, Australia, South Africa, California

Grape	Wine	Makes	Blended with	Grown
PINOT GRIGIO/ GRIS	White, sparkling	Varietals; Burgundy blends; Tokay-Pinot Gris (Alsace)	Chardonnay, Tokay	France (Alsace), Oregon, New Zealand (best); also Italy, France, Germany, Hungary, Romania
PINOT NOIR	Red, white, rosé, sparkling	Varietals: red Burgundy; Champagne (blanc de noirs)	Chardonnay, Pinot Meunier	France, New Zealand, Tasmania, USA; also Chile, South Africa
RIESLING	White, sparkling, sweet	Mainly varietals; sparkling (Sekt; Germany) dessert wines: Icewine (Canada), Eiswein (Germany)	Gewürztraminer, Sémillon, Sauvignon Blanc	Australia, Austria, Chile, France (Alsace), Germany, New Zealand, USA, South Africa, Canada
SANGIOVESE	Red	Brunello di Montalcino, Chianti	Cabernet Sauvignon, Merlot, Trebbiano	Italy (Tuscany); also California, Argentina, Chile
SAUVIGNON BLANC	White, sparkling, sweet	Varietals; Bordeaux blanc, Rueda, white Graves; Sancerre, Pouilly-Fumé; Fumé Blanc; Touraine; dessert wines (Sauternes, Monbazillac)	Sémillon; also Chardonnay, Riesling	Worldwide
SÉMILLON/ SEMILLON	White, sweet	Varietals; blends; white Graves; dessert wines (Sauternes, Barsac)	Chardonnay, Sauvignon Blanc	France, Australia; also Chile
SYRAH/SHIRAZ	Red, rosé, sparkling	Varietals; Languedoc, northern Rhône reds	Cabernet Sauvignon, Grenache/ Garnacha, Mourvèdre	Australia, France; also New Zealand, South Africa, USA, Spain, Chile, Switzerland
TEMPRANILLO	Red, fortified	Varietals; blends: Rioja, Ribera del Duero, other Spanish reds; Port	Garnacha (Grenache), Graciano, Mazuelo; also Cabernet Sauvignon	Spain; also Argentina, California, Portugal, southern France
TORRONTÉS	White	Varietals	N/A	Argentina
VIOGNIER	White	Varietals; Condrieu, Château-Grillet; also blends	Muscat, Roussanne, Syrah	France, California; also worldwide
ZINFANDEL	Red, rosé ('blush')	Varietals; Italian blends	As Primitivo, often blended with Negroamaro	California; also Italy (as Primitivo) and Australia

ß

Vitis vinifera *was spread throughout Europe, first by the Greeks and Phoenicians and later by the Romans. The Spanish brought* **Vitis vinifera** *to North and South America, the Dutch took it to South Africa, and the British introduced it – very politely, of course – to the Antipodes.*

WINES AROUND THE WORLD

When discussing the wines of the world, adopt the enigmatic air of a seasoned traveller. Channel your inner 'Man from Del Monte' and talk about vineyards as if you visit them regularly and viticulturists hang on your every word.

As you are no doubt well aware, winemaking is concentrated in two latitudinal bands encircling the globe. Most northern hemisphere wine regions are located between 32 and 51 degrees north, their southern counterparts between 28 and 42 degrees south. Global warming is benefiting the northern and southern extremes, such as England (52 degrees north) and Otago, New Zealand (46 degrees south), to the detriment of those nearer the equator.

The wine trade, uniquely, divides the globe into Old World (Europe) and New World (the colonies). You won't, for example, hear of BMW and Chrysler being described as Old World and New World cars – but you can remark that, of all the *Vitis* (grape) species found around the world, only the European *Vitis vinifera* is good enough for winemaking. Other species, especially the North American *Vitis labrusca*, impart a curiously 'foxy' quality to wine – not surprising, really, as it's called the 'fox grape'.

Vitis vinifera was spread throughout Europe, first by the Greeks and Phoenicians and later by the Romans. The Spanish brought *Vitis vinifera* to North and South America, the Dutch took it to South Africa, and the British introduced it – very politely, of course – to the Antipodes.

A monkey could make wine. In fact, monkeys do seek out fermenting fruits when in need of a buzz.

The creationist version has it that Noah planted the first vineyard: 'And he drank of the wine and was drunken; and he was uncovered within his tent.' (Well, we've all been there…) Non-creationists believe that wine was invented in Greece around the seventh century BC, and the French believe, naturally, that they perfected it.

Wine, as you know, is made naturally wherever wild, airborne yeasts come into contact with squashed grapes, converting sugar into alcohol. A monkey could make wine. In fact, monkeys do seek out fermenting fruits when in need of a buzz. The role of Man (especially the French) has been to refine the process – and how refined the French have made it.

France's gift to the wine world is the tortuous concept of *terroir*. The English gave cricket to the world and the rules of cricket are a lot simpler. In fact, *terroir* is so inscrutably Gallic that there is no equivalent word in English – which must please the French immensely. They probably consider it as payback for *le sandwich, le weekend* and *le shopping*. For bluffing purposes, though, you can describe *terroir* as the combined effect of soil, climate, topography and grape variety on wine. *Terroir* is what elevates mere plonk to fine wine, which, to the French mind, is an eloquent expression of a wine's place of origin. Advanced bluffers claim they can taste 'minerality' (hints of flint, chalk and limestone, etc.) in wines that truly express their *terroir*. Take your bluffing as far as you think you can safely take it.

Sceptics, however – and there are many – can't help noticing first, that it is *terroir* that makes wine expensive; second, that the French claim to have the best *terroir* in the world; and third, that French *terroir* can't be duplicated anywhere else. This *terroir* business would seem to be a win-win situation for the French. Only the dwindling market share of French wines indicates otherwise.

The concept of *terroir* is enshrined in the French system of *appellation contrôlée,* which dictates with brutal monomania which grape varieties may be planted where, how the vineyards must be tended and how the wine must be made in any given appellation. Its most extreme iteration is in Burgundy, where just a few rows of vines might be awarded their own appellation.

Most – but not all – French winemakers labour under this yoke, though ironically it is this inflexibility that has allowed New World winemakers to overtake them in the marketplace. Indeed, it is the very *absence* of such stifling rules and regulations that has enabled New World winemakers to experiment freely, to make wines we can understand and want to drink.

It's easy to bash the French, but there is one inescapable truth that even the most Francophobe ocker from the outback has to accept: France produces every major style of wine and these are still considered the international benchmarks. Consequently, New World winemakers are paying France the ultimate backhanded compliment by seeking out their own special sites and trying to identify the best grape varieties (usually French, of course) to grow there: *terroirism* by another name. This is happening just as the French are relaxing some of their rules with their *vin de pays* and *indication géographique protégée* (IGP) wine classifications. Think of these as *appellation contrôlée-lite,* allowing French winemakers some of the flexibility their competitors have enjoyed for years.

At this point you can beckon your adoring audience into the wonderful world of wine…

OLD WORLD

FRANCE: LES ROUGES (MAINLY)

Bordeaux

Confronted with a bottle of Bordeaux, you must, at the very least, express a preference for Left Bank or Right Bank. You might think it should be of no concern to others which way you swing (and you would probably be right), but there's kudos to be gained from aligning yourself with one side or the other.

We are, of course, talking about the left and right banks of the Gironde estuary, which bisects the Bordeaux region. Should you spot the words 'Médoc' or 'Graves' on the label, it's a Left Bank wine made predominantly from the lean, muscular Cabernet Sauvignon grape grown on well-drained gravelly soil. 'Graves', of course, is French – for 'gravelly soil'. If, on the other hand, it says 'St-Émilion', it will be a Right Bank wine made principally from the soft, approachable Merlot grape cultivated on (probably) calcareous clay. Wine buffs like words like 'calcareous'. And so, therefore, must you.

Express your preference according to whether you wish to be perceived as the strong-and-silent Cabernet Sauvignon type or a more touchy-feely Merlot kinda guy or gal. Be aware, too, that they also make white wines in Graves from Sauvignon Blanc and Sémillon, so do make sure the wine is red before announcing your allegiance to Left Bank or Right Bank, or you'll look a right twit.

Seasoned Bordeaux bluffers should also pass comment on the 1855 Bordeaux Wine Official Classification, whereby the top *châteaux* of the Médoc, and one in Graves, were ranked on an ascending scale of perceived quality running from *cinquièmes crus* or fifth growths at the bottom up to *premiers crus* or first growths at the top. For the benefit of your rapt audience, list the 1855 first growths as Château Lafite-Rothschild, Margaux, Latour, Mouton Rothschild and Haut-Brion (the one in Graves). Explain that these are officially the poshest wines in the world, adding that the Right Bank *châteaux* of Ausone, Cheval Blanc and Pétrus as well as d'Yquem in Sauternes (sweet white wine), are considered equally posh, albeit unofficially.

It might sound unpleasant, but think of 'growth' simply as an alternative word for vineyard, estate or *château*. Few are malignant, but you could argue that the 1855 classification is absurdly outdated, seeing as it was – and still is – based on the average prices fetched by the wines back in 1855. Roll your eyes at the unfairness of it all and say that some Bourgeois growths such as Chasse-Spleen, Poujeaux and Pibran are infinitely better than many top classed growths. Produce a little-known *château* from one of the Bordeaux satellite areas such as Bourg, Blaye or Côtes de Castillon and say it is just as good as many famous names. (Note the 'many', which does not commit you to dismissing them all.) It may not be, but it will certainly be one you can afford.

While d'Yquem is the most famous, and pricey, of the sweet Sauternes wines, you can go for the excellent Barsac, which is a good deal less expensive but often far more surprising and luscious.

Never be in awe of anything labelled 'Bordeaux *supérieur*' as the only thing *supérieur* about it is a slightly higher alcoholic strength than bog-standard Bordeaux. And always refer to red Bordeaux as 'claret'. When quizzed on your old-school pomposity, take care to explain that the whole region was under English rule in the twelfth century and that 'claret' is an anglicisation of *clairet*, meaning 'pale wine', which it is when compared with Spanish and Portuguese reds.

You could always take the line with Bordeaux that it no longer has much to do with wine, but much more to do with investment, insurance and finance. Many of the top *châteaux* are now owned by insurance or finance companies whose directors (and Chinese industrialists) are presumably among the few people able to afford the drink they produce. The classed growths are only too happy to accept the absurdly high prices the nouveau-riche Chinese are prepared to pay, squeezing traditional customers out of the market. Lament the fact that some *châteaux* also seem quite happy to dumb down their wines, forsaking backbone and elegance for riper, fruity styles to go with sweet-and-sour pork balls.

Burgundy

Strict adherence to Napoleonic inheritance laws, whereby estates are divided equally among each generation, has ensured that a map of Burgundy's vineyards resembles an intricate patchwork quilt, with many 'vineyards' amounting to no more than a couple of rows of vines. Locally, these tiny plots are known as *climats*, and each custodian protects his magic potion as fiercely as Asterix the Gaul protects his.

Burgundy, or *Bourgogne* if you're going native, is woefully complex to outsiders, but an understanding of the basics is essential for successful bluffing. The Côte d'Or, the heart of the region, is divided into two parts: the Côte de Nuits in the north makes red wines from Pinot Noir, while the Côte de Beaune to the south produces both Pinot Noir and white wines from the Chardonnay grape. The *grand crus* or top villages of the Côte de Nuits include Gevrey-Chambertin, Morey-St-Denis, Chambolle-Musigny, Vougeot and Vosne-Romanée, all of which make Pinot Noir. The *grand crus* in the Côte de Beaune include Puligny-Montrachet and Chassagne-Montrachet, which vie to produce the world's finest Chardonnays. All clear so far? Toss these names around like confetti to keep your audience on the back foot.

Introduce another layer of doubt by wondering aloud if Côte d'Or literally translates as 'golden slope', or whether it is an abbreviation of Côte d'Orient, a reference to the fact that this enormous escarpment faces east, thus catching the morning sun.

The most famous estate in Burgundy is the Domaine de la Romanée-Conti. It has a monopoly of some of

Burgundy's greatest vineyards (Romanée-Conti, La Tâche), but one's real awe and amazement should be reserved for the stratospheric prices the estate charges.

Unlike Bordeaux, where the reds are principally a blend of Cabernet Sauvignon and Merlot (the latter fleshing out the structure of the former) and the whites a blend of Sémillon and Sauvignon Blanc, Burgundy's wines are made almost exclusively from either Pinot Noir or Chardonnay. Refer to single-variety wines as *mono-cépage* if you're being fancy. Comment that Pinot Noir is notoriously fickle to cultivate – another factor in the enormous diversity of red Burgundy – and that Oregon and New Zealand are among the few places outside France where Pinot Noir has been coaxed to Burgundian heights.

Burgundy's 'other' white grape is the fairly astringent Aligoté, which is best drowned in cassis, as the locals drink it. This drink is, of course, a Kir, named after Canon Kir, who was mayor of Dijon and a hero of the French Resistance.

There are two approaches to take when discussing Burgundy. The first is a derisive chuckle: 'The Burgundians are living in the Middle Ages. The weather is atrocious, the winemaking techniques often faulty, the subdivision of properties a joke, the prices a scandal. Few people are gullible enough to buy most Burgundy.' The second approach is more indulgent. 'Yes, Burgundy is impossibly complicated, and the wines usually overpriced. But it is so rewarding. When you track down that obscure, perfect bottle, the pleasure is incomparable.'

Take your pick, but if you choose the latter, you will need to know some names. The line with Burgundy is that the grower is all-important. Lightly dismiss the big merchant houses (*négociants*) with the exceptions of Jadot, Joseph Drouhin and Louis Latour. Name the smart small *négociants*, Olivier Leflaive (of the same family as the famous but inconsistent Domaine Leflaive) and Verget. Drop into the conversation that in 1964 a quarter-bottle of Côte de Beaune was signed by all four Beatles and sold for £10,000.

End your discourse with a bombshell, quoting Anthony Hanson, a British Master of Wine and highly respected Burgundy expert, who famously wrote, 'Great Burgundy smells of shit.' When your audience has finished mopping red wine off their ties, explain that he meant this in a nice way and was simply referring to the farmyardy, wild-truffle aromas of the finest aged Pinot Noirs.

Beaujolais and Mâconnais

These regions are a southern extension of Burgundy, making some attractive red and white wines. It is a pity, therefore, that the wine most people still associate with Beaujolais is the over-acidic purple beverage known as Beaujolais Nouveau. Back in the 1970s, when shrimps were first discovered inside avocados and candles sprouted from Chianti flasks, Beaujolais Nouveau was the original 'cheeky little number'. The arrival of the new vintage on the third Thursday in November caused a right old kerfuffle. It was kind of fun while it lasted and fantastic for the region's cash flow, making a virtue of selling the current year's vintage when barely three months old. You, however, know that it is hopelessly unfashionable and that now less than a third of Beaujolais is sold as Nouveau.

If you must drink it, chill it and drink it quickly. Do not hang on to it for years and save it as an aged vintage; it will probably be thin and undrinkable. Remark that the predominant grape for Beaujolais is Gamay (see page 38) and because there's not a lot of tannin in this grape it won't keep for long. Tannins are the astringently dry-tasting chemical compounds that help to give structure and body to wine. This is why 'lean' wines can be as pleasurable as sucking an old tea bag.

Beaujolais to praise are the little-known village wines or the 10 Beaujolais *crus*, villages that would never stoop to churning out Nouveau. The lightest, softest and most floral of the Beaujolais *crus* – the ones most typical of the common perception of Beaujolais – come from the pretty villages of Chiroubles and Fleurie. Fuller-bodied Beaujolais comes from Brouilly, Côte de Brouilly, Juliénas, Régnié and St-Amour; the most structured, spiciest and long-lived Beaujolais (they can be aged for up to 10 years) come from the *crus* of Chénas, Morgon and Moulin-à-Vent, which is named after an old windmill.

The white Mâcon wines are the nearest non-millionaires can get to white Burgundy. The most famous of them is Pouilly-Fuissé. Among Mâcon-Villages there are two individual village names that are memorably odd: Mâcon-Prissé and Mâcon-Lugny (pronounced *loony*).

The Rhône

Being a long way from Paris, the North Sea and the Atlantic ports, the Rhône was ignored from the time of the Romans until around 1970. As a result, the powerful red wines, often a lot more enjoyable than most Bordeaux and Burgundy, were undervalued until a certain Robert Parker Jr (*see* Glossary, page 153) came and gave the game away. There are two things to remember. First of all, the Rhône, for wine purposes, is divided into north and south. Northern Rhône is expensive, exclusive and divided into small villages. Its red wines are made exclusively from the macho Syrah grape which is grown on vertiginous slopes. Southern Rhône is less expensive, less exclusive and divided into larger villages, like Châteauneuf-du-Pape. The landscape is much flatter here, and reds are a blend of mostly Grenache with Cinsault, Mourvèdre, Carignan and Syrah. Comment that the whole production of the northern Rhône is usually less than that of Châteauneuf-du-Pape, a single southern-Rhône appellation, which goes some way to explaining their eye-watering prices.

The second thing to remember is that the reds are much better than the whites, though important exceptions are the wines made from the Viognier grape: Condrieu, Château-Grillet in the north and one or two mavericks from the south such as Domaine Ste-Anne and Domaine Pélaquié.

The catch-all Côtes du Rhône appellation covers the vast swathe of vineyards in the southern Rhône, and is applied to undemanding wines, best drunk within five years while they're still reasonably fruity. The Côtes du

Rhône-Villages appellation is awarded to villages deemed to make stronger, more concentrated wines, and these can represent excellent value for money. Only the very best of the wines labelled Côtes du Rhône-Villages are entitled to use the actual name of the village: Côtes du Rhône-Villages Valréas, for example. Top village names to look out for include Cairanne, Laudun, Sablet and Séguret. Compared with bog-standard Côtes du Rhône, these wines are capable of ageing gracefully. The French refer to them as *vins de garde,* or 'keepers' to English speakers as in 'wine which will keep'. Drop that into conversation to cement your bluffing credentials. You will, of course, know that Côte-Rôtie ('roasted slope') and Hermitage are probably the best wines from the northern Rhône – full-bodied and rich – and that Paul Jaboulet is probably the best-known name for Hermitage. St-Joseph and Crozes-Hermitage (a less-strong, less-expensive form of Hermitage) are, depending on your point of view, either the poor relations or the only remotely affordable wines among northern Rhône reds. With Côte-Rôtie you can rhapsodise about Marcel Guigal's absurdly expensive single-vineyard bottlings, La Mouline, La Landonne and La Turque. No one can actually afford to buy these wines so you can say more or less anything you like about them without fear of challenge.

Châteauneuf-du-Pape is the name most people know. You might casually let slip that it is a blended wine; up to 13 grape varieties can be used, though Grenache and Syrah are predominant. Wax lyrical about the eccentrics of Châteauneuf-du-Pape, such as the wayward Henri Bonneau, who makes wonderful wines from a cellar resembling a medieval pigsty. And enthuse about the rare white Châteauneuf-du-Pape: quite heavy but well-worth finding.

With another famous southern Rhône wine, Beaumes-de-Venise, the thing to do is praise the lesser-known red rather than the more exposed sweet white Muscat. The Rhône also produces Tavel: truly a man's rosé.

The south of France

Traditionally, Languedoc-Roussillon was at the bottom of the stifling French wine hierarchy. To the educated Frenchman (from outside the region, obviously), it produced 'le plonk': decent enough for washing down peasant food like *cassoulet* and *bouillabaisse,* but nothing that could possibly grace the top table. You, of course, recognise the south as the most dynamic and exciting wine region in the whole of France, unfettered by the petty bureaucracy of *appellation contrôlée* rules, a rugged place where wild-haired, horny-handed winemakers do as they please. Refer to it as France's very own New World. Indeed, outside influences from as far afield as Australia have helped to shape the region's progressive attitudes to winemaking.

The lack of respect shown towards the south by the French wine establishment has been largely reciprocated by a 'couldn't give a monkey's' attitude towards the absurdly rigid *appellation contrôlée* rules. True enough, new appellations are springing up all over the south but some of the finest producers still prefer to label their wines as 'inferior' *vin de pays* or the more recent *Indication Géographique Protégée* (IGP), embracing the freedom to experiment that this allows. Some subregions – *sacré bleu!* – have been 'rewarded' with *grand cru* status, such as Berlou and Roquebrune, which make spicy reds in the St-Chinian appellation.

Should you find yourself drinking a spicy red Fitou in polite company, take a deep inhalation from the glass and exclaim, 'Ah, le Midi' (as this part of France is colloquially known), 'smell the wild herbs of the *garrigue:* rosemary and thyme – with a feral hint of goat?' (Okay, maybe the goat's overdoing it...)

Many of these wines are blends, the predominant local red grapes being Grenache, Carignan, Mourvèdre and Cinsault; whites include Grenache Blanc, Macabeo, Roussanne, Marsanne, Rolle, Clairette and Bourboulenc. Syrah and Cabernet Sauvignon are creeping into the red mix. Red appellations you should know about include St-Chinian, Fitou, Corbières, Minervois, Faugères and La Clape, all in the Languedoc, and Bandol in Provence. Please note: it is perfectly acceptable to like Bandol's manly rosés.

Top white appellations include St-Chinian, Clairette du Languedoc and La Clape, especially its very own *grand cru*, Pic-St-Loup. This is not to be confused with Picpoul de Pinet, which, you can casually mention, is a rarity in France: an appellation based on a single grape variety, in this case the lemon-scented Picpoul grape.

Should you see the words *vieilles vignes* on the label, it means that the wine is made from gnarly 'old vines', which are revered for their lower yields and, hence, greater concentration in their fruit. They like to draw attention to that in these parts.

FRANCE: LES BLANCS (MAINLY)

Chablis

Chablis is Burgundy's northernmost appellation, separated from the Côte d'Or by the Morvan hills. In fact, Chablis is nearer to the southern vineyards of Champagne than to Burgundy proper, and its wines were used occasionally in Champagne production up until the early 1900s. Traditional-style Chablis, aged in inert containers made of concrete or stainless steel, is probably the leanest, meanest, steeliest expression of Chardonnay, a million miles from the rich, buttery styles achieved by ageing Chardonnay in new oak. However, there has been a move by some producers towards oak-ageing Chablis with a view to softening its harder edges.

Look wistfully at the glass in your hand and adopt the stance of the purist for effect. Say, 'I do wish they'd stop corrupting Chablis with oak. It masks that incomparable *goût de pierre à fusil.*' This, of course, means 'taste of gunflint', which, we all know, is how to describe the mineral qualities of traditional Chablis.

And should you be fortunate enough to be present when someone makes a comment about Chablis's natural affinity with oysters, be sure to say, 'It's not really that surprising, considering that the roots of the vines reach down into Kimmeridgian clay and limestone containing layers of fossilised oyster shells – from the Upper Jurassic, I believe.' That's Olympic standard bluffing.

The Loire

The story of Loire wines is a long and winding tale of the riverbank, which will be useful for the bluffer to learn. The Continental climate in the Upper Loire produces tangy, gooseberry-ish Sauvignon Blanc in Sancerre and Pouilly-Fumé, the template for New Zealand's brasher world-beaters. *Fumé*, meaning 'smoked', describes the odd whiff of gunflint emanating from these wines (*see* Chablis, opposite), which here comes from flinty soils called silex. On no account confuse Pouilly-Fumé with Pouilly-Fuissé, which, as you know, comes from Mâconnais in Burgundy and is made from Chardonnay.

The maritime climate in the Pays Nantais, where the Loire spills into the Atlantic, produces the famous 'fish wine', Muscadet, which is made from the rather neutral Melon de Bourgogne grape. One of the best-kept secrets in wine is that Muscadet doesn't taste of anything to speak of (it's extremely hard to identify in blind tastings). This is why some of the tastier examples are matured *sur lie*, which means the wines are kept in contact with their lees (sediment of dead yeast cells, bits of pips, skin and stems) over the winter months in a bid to add a little body and flavour. It also gives the wine a little spritz, a quality the French describe (you will remember) as *pétillant* (slightly sparkling). You should also be aware that *pétillant* falls between *perlant* (only a little bit sparkling) and *mousseux* (very sparkling). 'Fizzy' is just not good enough for a practised bluffer, and it cannot be stressed enough that the word is to be avoided. While still in the Pays Nantais, steer clear of the brutally acidic Gros Plant wines if you value your tooth enamel.

What can one say about the wines of the middle Loire? Or, more importantly, what can *you* say about them? How about: 'Nowhere else in France produces so many styles of wine from such a diverse cornucopia of grape varieties.' These include the Cabernets Franc and Sauvignon, Gamay, Chardonnay, Malbec, Pinot Noir, Pinot Gris and the Loire workhorse grape, Chenin Blanc.

With a reputation for making achingly boring wines all around the world, Chenin shines in the middle Loire (Anjou, Saumur, Touraine). Not so much Chenin Blanc as Chameleon Blanc, it makes every style of white – still and sparkling, dry and sweet in every combination – but you know that the best are the dry Savennières from Anjou, *demi-sec* or medium Vouvray from Touraine, and the sweet Bonnezeaux and Quarts de Chaume, both from Côteaux du Layon in Anjou.

There's some good bluffing potential to be had from the red wines in this predominantly white-wine region. The Loire is pretty much the northern limit for red winemaking (mad dogs and Englishmen take note), producing light, elegant wines. The best of these are Chinon and Bourgueil, which are made from the Cabernet Franc grape, the latter being as close to Ribena as you can get without infringing the patent. You know, of course, that these are best served lightly chilled.

The vintage should usually be the latest or the one before that. Conversely, with the sweet wines, the older the better. And while discussing vintages, comment on the Loire's wide vintage variation, owing to its marginal winemaking climate.

Alsace

Here you must always refer to the wines as 'from Alsace' for, as the great wine writer André Simon once remarked, 'Alsatian is ze dog.'

Alsace has been shunted backwards and forwards between France and Germany so many times that it's no wonder it can't really make up its mind whether it is German or French. Accordingly, it has opted for some of both, but unfortunately it has taken the steeliness of German wines and the pricing of the French. Comment on the distinctively Germanic tall, elegant 'flute' bottles adopted by the region, as opposed to the tall-shouldered Bordeaux-style bottles or sloping-shouldered Burgundy bottles used in other parts of France.

The main grape varieties in Alsace are Gewurztraminer (remember, here it drops the umlaut) and Riesling, Pinot Gris and Pinot Blanc. *Gewürz* is German for 'spice'. Open a bottle and get that aroma of a perfume factory full in the face. Hugel is probably the biggest producer and the most well-known.

Apart from the courtesan's boudoir of Gewurz, there is the intense muskiness of Pinot Gris (called Tokay-Pinot-Gris in Alsace, although it has no connection with Hungarian Tokay) and the pure grapey-ness of Muscat, which you fully expect to be sweet but finishes bone-dry. Local legend says that the variety originally came from Hungary, but this isn't likely. And for another paradox, enthuse about Alsace Pinot Noir, the only red wine made in this white-wine territory.

Alsace wines used to be remarkably simple and clear, Alsace being the only French region where it is a requirement to name the grape variety on the label. Then they introduced a fiendish hierarchy of *grands crus* (named vineyards) to run alongside the grape varieties. Now everyone is thoroughly confused, but at least the growers can charge higher prices. All rather like Burgundy, in fact.

THE OTHER MAIN EUROPEAN CONTENDERS

Italy

If you consider what the Italians have done to coffee – there's *ristretto*, *macchiato* and *affogato* before we even get to boring old *latte, espresso* and *cappuccino* – just imagine what they can do to wine. Italian wine is so complicated and disorganised that even Italian wine experts are bluffing. It's a giant 'bunga bunga' party featuring nearly 1,000 grape varieties and hundreds of new regions that no one outside Italy has ever heard of. Embrace this bluffer's paradise.

Italy produces more wine than any other country, but also more indifferent wine than any other country. Some Italian wine is delicious, but like the better Swiss and Austrian wines very little of this is exported. The Italians, quite understandably, prefer to drink it themselves. You should remember that people are very sentimental about Italy and allow themselves to believe that just because the country is beautiful, the wines must be good, too – and Italian restaurateurs have taken full advantage of this weakness.

The first bandwagon you should jump on has 'Super

Tuscan' written down the side. Super Tuscans are not absurdly good-looking people who bomb about the countryside in Maseratis, but wines made by absurdly good-looking people who bomb about the countryside in Maseratis. Some even wear their underpants over their trousers. Toss around names like Ornellaia, Sassicaia, Solaia and Tignanello as confidently as if you were tossing pasta. These are the original and most famous of the Super Tuscan wines.

The movement started in the late 1960s as a protest against the rigid and often nonsensical rules of the *Denominazione di Origine Controllata* (DOC) classification for Italian wines. Like the French *appellation contrôlée* system, it lays down the law with regard to which grape varieties, vine-husbandry techniques and winemaking methods can be used in each region in order for a wine to earn official DOC status. The Super Tuscan winemakers decided they would rather forsake DOC status if it meant they could bend the rules, using foreign grape varieties like Cabernet Sauvignon and Merlot, for example. This is why some of Italy's finest and most expensive wines are labelled as bog-standard *vino da tavola* (table wine) which, like the French *vin de pays* classification, allows winemakers a great deal more flexibility and innovation. More recently, the equally flexible *Indicazione Geografica Tipica* or IGT category has been introduced to spare some of Italy's top producers the indignity of labelling their wines as *vino da tavola*. Observe that the Super Tuscan movement is mushrooming (*funghi*-ing?) these days, resulting in some not-so-Super Tuscans.

We all know that Chianti's traditional straw-covered

fiasco bottles make a perfectly charming lamp stand, but did you know that Chianti's principal grape is Sangiovese, Italy's most widely planted variety? It is permissible for Chianti to contain 20% other grapes, which modernists take full advantage of, fleshing out their wines with Cabernet Sauvignon and Merlot. Purists stick with mainly Sangiovese, with perhaps a dash of local Canaiolo. You could express a preference for the latter style because you're particularly fond of the slightly savoury character of traditional Italian reds as opposed to overtly fruity – more sun-dried tomatoes than blackcurrants.

Obviously, you're aware that Piemonte is the home of big, bruising Barolo wines made from the Nebbiolo grape, as well as the much lighter Barbera wine which, owing to its notably high acidity, is a fantastic 'food wine' – perfect with pizza/pasta, etc.

The other Italian regions with positive bluffing potential are located in the south, especially Puglia and the islands of Sardinia and Sicily. Again, drawing parallels with France, southern Italy traditionally produced macho reds and simple whites, but massive investment in new equipment, reduction of grape yields and the introduction of alien grape varieties have transformed the south into the most happening Italian region.

Seek out newly fashionable white wines made from Falanghina, Grillo, Vermentino and Inzolia, and burly reds from Nero d'Avola, Negroamaro ('black-bitter') and Primitivo. Foreign grapes putting down roots in the south include Syrah/Shiraz, Cabernet Sauvignon, Chardonnay and Viognier. All Sicilian wines are absolutely flawless and magnificent, and that observation has nothing to do with a recent visit to the Bluffer's Guides HQ from a charming gentleman called Vito and his business associate Rocco. A little-known fact to disseminate is that Bob Dylan has joined the ranks of celebrity wine growers and has a vineyard in Marche, producing 'Planet Waves' (after his 1974 album), which has been described as a 'mysteriously Dylanesque encounter between the severity of Montepulciano and the softness of Merlot'. Such is the glamorous allure of *la dolce vita* that Mick Hucknall of Simply Red has joined His Bobness, producing a wine on Mount Etna called – no, not Simply Red, but 'Il Cantante' ('The Singer'). Sting, meanwhile, has an estate near Florence where he makes wines called 'Casino delle Vie' and 'Sister Moon': organic and biodynamic, of course, but probably tantric, too.

Spain

In wine circles it is now compulsory to refer to the 'New Spain'; plain old 'Spain' will no longer suffice. Indeed, the 'new' word is now as tenaciously attached to Spain as it is to Zealand, York and Romney. You need to know why.

In a nutshell, red Rioja has dominated the Spanish wine scene so effectively for so long that a proliferation of new and exciting wine regions (*Denominación de Origens* or DOs) is truly shaking things up. Today the Spanish wine map is being constantly redrawn to accommodate newly classified regions where can-do winemakers are asserting their regional heritage via suddenly fashionable local grape varieties. And what's more, they're making their wines differently.

This is quite a generalisation, but they are challenging Spain's traditional, macho preoccupation with extended ageing in musty old barrels which invariably produces tired, oxidised, heavily tannic wines with little grape aroma. Instead, they're installing squeaky-clean stainless-steel equipment, ensuring a faster turnover of barrels and bottling earlier to make modern, elegant styles where fruit and terroir aren't buried beneath layers of old wood. They are, quite literally, taking a fresh approach.

Spain is such a hotbed of viticultural experimentation right now that you could safely describe it as the most New World of Old World countries (as opposed to South Africa, which is the most Old World of New World countries). Hot regional/wine names to drop include: Priorat/Priorato in Catalonia, where Garnacha and Cariñena grapes are mixing with Cabernet Sauvignon; Somontano in the Pyrenean foothills, where red varieties Parraleta and Moristel are joined by Chardonnay and Gewürztraminer; Toro to the west of Valladolíd for beefy, tannic reds from Garnacha and Tinta de Toro (a regional variant of Tempranillo); and Bierzo in Castilla y León, where they're coaxing wonders from the local red Mencía grape.

Mention Galicia on the northwest Atlantic coast as the epicentre for excellent Spanish white wines. This windswept, rain-lashed, atypically green region is Spain's answer to Cornwall or Brittany, with a strong Celtic influence evidenced by the Galicians' predilection for pasties (*empanadas*) and bagpipes. Extol the peachy, aromatic virtues of Albariño made in Rías Baixas, taking care to pronounce it *REE-ass BY-shahss*, which cannot fail to impress. Add that Albariño is, in fact, the Spanish name for Portugal's Alvarinho, one of the grapes used to make tooth-stripping Vinho Verde just over the border to Galicia's south. Albariño is arguably Spain's most fashionable white grape, but it's looking anxiously over its shoulder at Godello from Monterrei, Galicia's newest wine zone. Satisfyingly obscure, you can describe Godello as similar to Albariño but with a slightly softer mouth-feel. How about 'the New Albariño', or is this just getting silly?

Even white Rioja has changed in that Chardonnay, Sauvignon Blanc and Verdejo are now sometimes blended with the traditional Viura. 'New Wave' white Rioja is made in a fresh, fruity style with minimum use of oak, allowing you to deplore the virtual disappearance of old-fashioned oak-aged white Rioja with its rounded, nutty flavours. It is the bluffer's prerogative to be inconsistent.

In fact, you can be downright perverse. Allege that red Rioja has become unpredictable: either 'too oaky' or 'not oaky enough', according to your whim. You know that Rioja's trademark characteristic is its sweetish, vanilla quality produced by ageing in American oak. Point out that subtler French oak is increasingly being used and that more than half of Rioja's reds are sold young with no oak ageing at all.

The principal grape variety in red Rioja is Tempranillo blended with a little Garnacha. You also need to know about Rioja's quality ladder: if you spot the words *sin crianza* ('without ageing') or *joven* ('young') on the label, then the wine has barely been aged at all; *crianza* means it has had two years, the first in oak; *reserva* has an extra year in bottle; and *gran reserva* has the benefit of at least two years in oak and three in bottle.

Navarra used to be considered a poor relation of Rioja, but you should say it is now far better value. Praise the sanctioning by the Spanish authorities of the inclusion of the French Cabernet Sauvignon grape: recall that, in the nineteenth century, Spanish paranoia about French invasions reached such a pitch that the railway gauge was changed at the border.

Portugal

Many casual wine drinkers know little of Portuguese wine beyond Port, its great fortified wine, and maybe Mateus Rosé. You, however, are aware that Portuguese table wines are a cure for palate fatigue, offering a welcome alternative to the me-too Cabernet Sauvignons and identikit Chardonnays strangling the wine world with their far-reaching tendrils.

Geographically isolated on the western Atlantic fringe of Europe and rather strapped for cash (until EU grants flooded in), Portuguese winemakers have persisted with their own grape varieties – even the ones with hard-to-love names like Borrado das Moscas ('Fly Droppings') and Bastardo (um, 'Bastard'). Impress friends and enemies alike by announcing that Portugal's trump card is its unique range of indigenous grapes. It probably has about 300 native varieties, you could add, of which some 50 are widely grown. In fact, one still encounters 'field blends', which is a term for vineyards with as many as 20 or 30 grape varieties mixed together, though this is becoming less common as Portugal's growers experiment with 'site selection' to find the best combinations of grape and soil type. Yes, international (by which we mean 'French') grape varieties are creeping into Portuguese vineyards, but this is not the main story with Portuguese wines.

Announce that you're partial to the big, tannic reds from the Douro Valley (where Port comes from) which are made from traditional Port grapes. List these as Touriga Nacional (the most important), Touriga Franca, Tinta Cão, Tinta Barroca, Touriga Francesa and Tinta Roriz – which is Rioja's Tempranillo. Explain that Touriga Nacional usually provides the backbone, its aggressive, tannic tendencies curbed through blending. When made into table wines, the result is rich and spicy, dark and brooding: a bit like unfortified Port, funnily enough.

And please remember that no reference to the Douro Valley is complete without alluding to its 'rugged, timeless beauty'. Though you'll probably be pushing it if you claim you can taste the valley's pre-Cambrian schist in its wines.

The yin to the Douro's yang is the almost water-white Vinho Verde wine from the northern province of Minho. Vinho Verde means 'green wine', but this doesn't have anything to do with its colour. It refers, of course, to its fresh, youthful, slightly under-ripe style. These zippy whites are made from the Trajadura, Arinto and Alvarinho grapes – the latter, as you know, being the Portuguese name for Spain's achingly fashionable Albariño.

With regard to Portugal's up-and-coming wine regions, name-check the Dão region (pronounced somewhere between *dow* and *dung*), primarily known for its robust red wines; and Alentejo, which is the source of most of the world's wine corks. Should anyone express a fondness for the cheap-and-cheerful wines of Estremadura, immediately correct them, pointing out that this Atlantic coastal region to the north of Lisbon is now called Lisboa, the source of fresh, aromatic whites, including Chardonnay, and rich, spicy reds from Cabernet Sauvignon, Syrah, Castelão, Touriga Nacional and Aragonez which is – altogether now – another name for Spain's Tempranillo.

Not to be outdone by Italy's celebrity winemakers, Portugal has attracted Sir Cliff Richard to the Algarve, where he spends his time playing tennis, looking suspiciously young and supervising winemakers. You might try claiming that you're a regular visitor to Adega do Cantor (or 'Winery of the Singer') in which case you'll need to know that his wine is called 'Vida Nova' (stealing a march on Ricky Martin, should the Latino heart-throb ever turn his considerable talents to wine).

Greece

The informed bluffer knows that there is more to Greek wine than Retsina. We've all brought a bottle home from holiday only to find that it just doesn't taste the same on a wet Wednesday in Cricklewood as it did outside a *taverna* with the Aegean licking our toes. Gone is the lemon and pine freshness, replaced by the aroma of pine-scented Toilet Duck – proving that most cheap holiday wines taste better *in situ*.

Retsina is made principally from the Savatiana grape, which is prized for its exceptional drought-resistance.

Mention the Greek winemaker (you forget his name) who explained that most producers now tone down the pine impact of their Retsinas for the benefit of younger Greeks and for most export markets – but that they crank it up for Germany, their biggest export market.

Bluffers can have a ball with Greece because if you declare a soft spot for Xynomavro from Goumenissa or Moschofilero from Mantinia, no one (Greeks excluded) will have a clue what you're on about. The Greeks, who actually invented wine, provide you with a lexicon of exotic, unfamiliar words you can toss about with gay abandon (something else the Greeks invented). And most of the labels are written in Greek, too, so there is little chance of being found out as you drop these polysyllabic word bombs. Talk about the rapidly modernising wine industry and how Greek winemaking culture is becoming less insular as more of its winemakers broaden their horizons in places like France and Germany.

Obviously, the two most widely planted red grapes are Agiorgitiko and the aforementioned Xynomavro. Point out that one should expect a wide variation in style from fresh and young to rich and spicy with Agiorgitiko, adding that it blends most pleasingly with Cabernet Sauvignon. With Xynomavro (the name means 'acid black'), explain that it can seem harsh in youth but ages well, becoming softer as it matures.

As with all wines cultivated in very hot climates where fruit can become over-ripe, Greek wines, especially the reds, sometimes struggle to achieve much acidity. Which is why Greek winemakers covet the cool-climate growing conditions found at high altitude, especially on north-facing slopes.

Reserve your childlike enthusiasm for the remarkable white wines made from the Assyrtiko grape on the volcanic Greek island of Santorini. A cataclysmic eruption in 1614 BC showered the island with ash and lava, which imparts a minerally, slightly salty tang to these citrusy wines. Assyrtiko might sound like the name of a 1970s American cop show, but it is the last word in crisp, fresh summer drinking.

Germany

Don't make the common mistake of dismissing all German wines as unfashionable sugar-water. Confident bluffers know better than this, aware that Riesling is the darling white grape of the cognoscenti. They wax lyrical about Riesling's tantalising, knife-edge balance between richness and rapier-like acidity, so there's no reason why you shouldn't join in. The acclaimed wine writer Hugh Johnson himself calls Riesling 'the greatest and most versatile wine grape of all' – and he would be Professor Dumbledore at the Hogwarts School of Wine Writing, if there were such a thing.

Be aware that fine, aged Riesling often has flavours of petrol and kerosene, but this is A Good Thing. If stumped for an adjective, call it 'racy', and for heaven's sake, remember to pronounce it *REE-zling*, not *RYE-zling*, which means instant social death in wine circles.

German wines often have a distinctive sweetness, but you must not fall into the philistine trap of condemning all sweet wines. Puddings, *pâtisserie* and fruit are sweet, so why shouldn't some wines be the equivalent of the dessert rather than the main course? Germany's great dessert wines – i.e., Auslese, Trockenbeerenauslese and Eiswein – uniquely are not really pudding wines (they don't have enough alcohol) but wines that are a dessert in themselves. One sip of Trockenbeerenauslese is probably equivalent to a whole slice of Sachertorte. But for all this talk of sugar, German Riesling is often as low as 8.5% abv, which means about 80 calories a glass. Practise saying, 'I use Zeltinger Himmelreich Riesling Kabinett Halbtrocken as part of my calorie-controlled diet.'

Meanwhile, the Germans have started to make a lot of their wines *trocken* (dry) or *halbtrocken* (half-dry), but no matter how *trocken,* they are still more astringent than dry. These take a bit of getting used to, but go well with food. They are an excellent bluffing area because few people seem to be aware of their existence.

Not so long ago, German wine had sunk so low in public esteem that some producers even resorted to Australian-style names and labels (like Windy Ridge) in an attempt to market it. The culprit was, of course, Liebfraumilch – literally, 'Virgin Mary's Milk' – a product hardly known in its land of origin. A possible line of interest here is to praise the 'real' Liebfraumilch: the wine from the tiny Liebfrauen-Stiftskirche vineyard next to Worms Cathedral. 'Unfortunately, it's practically unobtainable,' you can add smugly.

In keeping with the Germans' need for order, their wine is governed by the world's most complex, but apparently logical, grading system. Declare that the whole system is in fact totally illogical (more or less true) and should be scrapped. This should give you a legitimate excuse for not knowing anything about it, but in case you are interrogated just remember it's a five-rung quality ladder based on ascending levels of natural grape sugars: essentially a scale of sweetness. From the bottom up, now, repeat after me: Kabinett, Spätlese ('late harvest'), Auslese ('selected harvest'), Beerenauslese (made from individually selected berries) and, the sweetest, Trockenbeerenauslese (mercifully abbreviated to TBA).

Good luck.

Austria

Since the antifreeze scandal of 1985, when a few bad apples sweetened up their late-harvest wines with a dash of diethylene glycol, the Austrian wine industry has reinvented itself, almost from scratch, as a source of beautifully crafted boutique wines made from some of the world's most interesting grape varieties. These provide top bluffing potential for the post-Chardonnay, post-Cabernet winebibber.

Go into ecstasies about Grüner Veltliner, Austria's most important native white grape, at its best in the Kamptal, Kremstal and Wachau regions. Comment knowingly on its typical white-pepper spiciness (or lack of if you've got a dud one) and how it's usually at its best served young and fresh – or *heurige*, as they say in the Viennese taverns of the same name. Also express an admiration for the tingling, fresh Sauvignon Blancs from Styria.

Extol the trademark acidity of Blaufränkisch, the most widely planted native red grape. Explain that the best examples come from Burgenland, occasionally blended with Cabernet Sauvignon and Pinot Noir. It's safe to describe this wine as 'racy' – unless of course its freshness has been obliterated by the heavy-handed use of new oak, a practice you deplore.

The Wachau region is also home to top-class Rieslings which, you can say, have more in common with aromatic Alsace Rieslings than their zippy German counterparts. Do point out that the white grape known as Welschriesling is no relation, and that it doesn't even come from Wales. *Welsch* in this case simply means 'foreign'.

Most Welschriesling is made into light, dryish whites for early drinking, but its piercing acidity also comes in handy for balancing the extraordinary sweetness of Austria's famous late-harvest wines. These are made on the shores of the enormous Neusiedler See (lake) in Burgenland, where autumn mists promote the onset of botrytis. Also known as 'noble rot', this benevolent fungus dehydrates grapes, concentrating their sugar content. Top producers include Alois Kracher and Willi Opitz, who issued a CD of grapes fermenting in a vat. Sadly, you left your copy in the car…

Eastern Europe

What to say about Eastern Europe, now that the tidal wave of cheap Bulgarian Cabernet Sauvignon and Hungarian Bull's Blood has been reduced to a trickle? In the 1980s, these cheerful, gluggable reds were as big as Alexis Carrington's shoulder pads, but alas: no more. Foreign investment and winemakers have poured in with varying success. They've been trying to beat New World wine countries at their own game with affordable, understandable wines (labelled by variety, sometimes with anglicised names), but regional politics haven't always been conducive to export, and quality has been like Forrest Gump's box of chocolates. The best line to take is a condescending 'Quality is improving with each vintage.' It works for wine writers, so it's worth a punt.

On the downside, many interesting indigenous grape varieties have been lost in an eternal sea of Cabernet Sauvignon, Merlot, Pinot Noir, Pinot Gris and Chardonnay. Demonstrate your knowledge of Eastern European grapes by name-checking plummy Mavrud and Melnik (Bulgarian reds); Feteasc Neagr (the black maiden) and Feteasc Alb (the white maiden) from Romania; and, from Hungary, Irsai Oliver, Furmint and Hárslevelü (mainly dry whites), and Kardaka and Kékfrankos for reds. Remind your adoring listeners that Kékfrankos and Austria's Blaufränkisch are one and the same.

Should anyone venture that Bull's Blood is Hungary's most famous wine, reply in your most patient bedside manner that this might once have been the case among hard-up students looking for a favourable grant/ alcohol exchange rate, but among the cognoscenti it has to be Tokaji (pronounced *Tock-eye*). As you know, this illustrious dessert wine graced the court of every European despot, earning it the title 'wine of kings and king of wines'. It's made from botrytised Furmint and Hárslevelü grapes.

As for Bull's Blood, insist on using the local name, which is Bikaver. Tell the amusing tale of the siege of Eger in 1552(ish), when Turkish invaders convinced themselves that the local plonk must surely contain bull's blood. How else to explain the strength and resolve of the castle's defenders before chickening out and going home? Bikaver, of course, was traditionally made from the ancient Kadarka grape but now contains Kékfrankos and the usual suspects of international grape varieties.

Romanian Pinot Noir, which sounds about as probable as Irish caviar, is a wine to mention, and certainly to buy when you're hard up.

England

While the English are renowned for their sense of humour (Monty Python, Benny Hill, Charlie Drake *et al*), the line to take with English wines is that they're just not funny any more – well, not the sparkling wines, anyway. In fact, English fizz now regularly beats Champagne in blind tastings, an achievement the English are keen to advertise with uncharacteristic brashness.

The secret to this sparkling success is simple: the chalk and limestone soils in England's southern downlands, iconically represented by the White Cliffs of Dover, are geologically identical to those in Champagne, and the climates are not too dissimilar, though Champagne has much colder winters. Both are classified as 'cool-climate' wine regions, producing grapes with high acidity, which are perfect for sparkling-wine production.

Champagne producers, most notably Louis Roederer, maker of Cristal, have been spotted sniffing around the southern English countryside, where land prices can be 20 times cheaper than in Champagne.

Point out that the English are hardly new to this winemaking lark. The Romans introduced viticulture to England, where it prospered until the double whammy of a cooling climate and Henry VIII's decision to dissolve the monasteries, which is where most of the vines were cultivated (a useful historical reference for wine bluffers). This time around, climate change (global warming) is working in England's favour.

Do mention Denbies in Surrey, Coates & Seely in Hampshire, and Ridgeview and Nyetimber, both in Sussex, as English wineries making quintessentially English fizz but doing so by using French techniques and the classic Champagne grape varieties (Chardonnay, Pinot Noir and Pinot Meunier) grown in Champagne-esque chalky soil. Point out that Camel Valley in Cornwall also manages to produce top-class fizz on sandy soils. And comment on the fruit-forward, floral qualities of English sparkling wine ('You can almost smell the hedgerows' – that sort of thing) as opposed to the more yeasty, biscuity qualities of Champagne.

As fiercely proud as they are of their products, the yeomen winemakers of England are struggling to come up with a catchier name than 'English sparkling wine'. Some have suggested a Franglais word, 'Britagne' (pronounced *Britannia*). Others have suggested Merret, after Christopher Merret, who you will recognise as the Englishman who discovered the traditional method for making sparkling wines before Dom Pérignon popped his cork and took all the glory.

Urge your friends to treat English red wines with caution, however. Point out that the Champenois do grow two red-grape varieties, Pinot Noir and Pinot Meunier, for Champagne production, but they're not fool enough to make red wines out of them.

NEW WORLD

THE AMERICAS

USA

Should any discussion of American wines veer beyond your bluffing comfort zone, simply invoke the Judgment of Paris. The most seismic date in modern wine history is 24 May 1976: the day the nobility of French viticulture met its Agincourt. You can replace the plucky English archers with two unflinching rows of California Chardonnay and Cabernet Sauvignon, but the results were horribly similar.

Tell the amusing tale of how British wine merchant Steven Spurrier organised a blind tasting in the French capital, pitching California Chardonnay against the aristocracy of Burgundy, and California Cabernet against the might of Bordeaux. You can see what's coming, can't you? Stag's Leap Cabernet Sauvignon and Chateau Montelena Chardonnay, both 1973 and as Californian as *Baywatch*, came top in their respective tastings, beating the likes of Château Haut-Brion 1970 and Roulot Meursault-Charmes 1973. *Quelle horreur!* And to really rub salt into the wounds, the tasters were *grands fromages* of the French wine establishment.

The same results today wouldn't raise an eyebrow, but in 1976, just a year before *Star Wars*, French viticulture regarded itself as the Death Star, unassailable and impregnable. In France, the results were dismissed as laughable, although they were seized upon as a great source of encouragement for winemakers, not just in the USA, but throughout the New World – and the French have been paying the price ever since. Of course, they demanded a rematch of the very same wines, on the grounds that the French wines would age better. This took place in San Francisco in 1978, and the winners, again, were Californian – just as they were yet again in 2006 in the Judgment's 30th-anniversary tasting, held simultaneously in London and Napa, California. Sometimes it's just best to stop digging.

Seeking to console his French chums, Steven Spurrier commented, 'The results of a blind tasting cannot be predicted and will not even be reproduced the next day by the same panel tasting the same wines.' Which rather raises the question: what's the point? But, of course, this is music to the bluffer's ears.

From Texas to Hawaii, from sea to shining sea, wine is made in all 50 of these United States of America – that's if you include some nutters up in Alaska making it from salmonberries. But 95% comes from California, making it the fourth-largest wine producer in the world, after Italy, France and Spain. This sort of global economic insight is wine bluffing gold.

The bulk of California wine comes from the 483km-long Central Valley, where irrigated vines churn out nothing special. But in Lodi, to the north of the valley, they're making seriously good, great-value wines from Zinfandel, which was proclaimed 'America's Heritage Grape' by the ZAP group (Zinfandel Advocates and Producers). As a bluffer, it's your duty to point out that DNA testing in 1994 revealed this 'all-American grape' to be none other than southern Italy's Primitivo, an association the Italians have dined out on ever since.

As you are well aware, Zinfandel makes a wide range of wine styles from sweet, pale-pink wines at around 11% abv (referred to either as 'blush' wines or, confusingly, White Zinfandel) all the way up to dark, tannic monsters with notes of cinnamon, black pepper and cloves with as much as 17% abv. The undisputed King of Zin is Paul Draper, who makes intense, old-vine wines at Ridge Vineyards up in the Santa Cruz Mountains.

North of San Francisco, Napa Valley is the focal point for expensive, top-quality California wines. Most of the classic French grapes are grown here, but Cabernet Sauvignon is head honcho, either neat or in Bordeaux-style blends (principally with Merlot) referred to as 'Meritage'. Like most of California's northern coastal areas, the Napa Valley is cooled by Pacific breezes and by morning fog rolling in off the ocean. The valley sides offer cooler, high-altitude growing conditions.

Appropriately, 'Napa' derives from a Native American word meaning 'plenty' because in Napa nothing exceeds like excess. Its wines are like Hollywood teeth: huge, unnervingly bright and faintly unbelievable. Napa is also the epicentre of California's cult-wine phenomenon, a quasi-religion built upon big, brooding Cabernets with lush, black fruit and firm tannins.

Cult status is usually conferred by 'the world's most influential wine critic', Robert Parker Jr (aka 'The Million Dollar Nose'), who rates wines on a 100-point scale. For example, he awarded 99 points to the 1992 vintage of Screaming Eagle, single bottles of which can be bought online for £4,600. Consequently, these wines are often bought as futures (i.e., before they're bottled) and collected as trophies. Few would be gauche enough to actually drink them.

Napa's wines are like Hollywood teeth: huge, unnervingly bright, and faintly unbelievable.

There really must be something in the soil in Oakville, Napa, the home of Screaming Eagle, the similarly revered Harland Estate, and Opus One, the stellar Bordeaux blend assembled by the late legendary Robert Mondavi and Baron Philippe de Rothschild. Other cult wines to name-check include Araujo, Marcassin, Switchback Ridge and Scarecrow.

Napa Valley is also the name of the region's American Viticultural Area or AVA, which is a bit like the French *appellation contrôlée* system. You should argue, however, that the valley comprises so many diverse soils and microclimates that this blanket term is rendered meaningless. An AVA is no guarantee of quality; it merely requires that 85% of the grapes in a wine come from the specified AVA.

You might gently suggest that Napa has become somewhat overexposed, and better value is to be found in the neighbouring Sonoma district, where they make excellent Cabernet Sauvignon, Chardonnay, Zinfandel, and Merlot, which seems to have survived the post-*Sideways* backlash. Quote the classic line 'I am NOT drinking any f***ing Merlot!' from this seminal 2004 'wine tour' film. Sonoma's Russian River Valley subregion produces cool-climate Pinot Noir, Chardonnay and top-class fizz.

Incidentally, some of California's best sparkling wines are made by Schramsberg (Napa); Domaine Chandon, a Napa Valley venture of the Moët & Chandon Champagne house; Gloria Ferrer, built by Spain's Freixenet company in Carneros; and Roederer Estate, another Champagne outpost, this time in Anderson Valley in northernmost Mendocino. Roederer's rosé is particularly good.

As to California's top Chardonnays, these include Napa's age-worthy Chateau Montelena (of Judgment of Paris fame) and Kistler Vineyards in Russian River ('which is showing more restraint these days, don't you find?')

Should your host offer you a glass of Californian wine, do enquire whether he or she has tried any wines from the Pacific Northwest, by which you mean Oregon and Washington State. Oregon's long, cool autumns provide perfect ripening conditions for Burgundy's temperamental Pinot Noir – so good, in fact, that Burgundy wine merchant Robert Drouhin felt inspired to set up Domaine Drouhin here in 1987. He chose the Willamette Valley, which is now the source of silky, elegant Pinot Noirs that are a match for similarly priced Burgundies. Chardonnay, Riesling and Pinot Gris also fare well in Oregon. Moving inland, east of the Cascade Mountains, Washington State becomes an arid dustbowl, where irrigated valleys make intensely fruity Cabernet Sauvignon, Syrah and Chardonnay, and some of the finest Merlot on the West Coast.

If your host is familiar with these wines, make a tactical switch to the East Coast. Ask if he or she has tried the dry Rieslings of New York State, from the Finger Lakes area in particular.

Chile

An unfeasibly long and narrow strip of land, measuring 4,300km north to south but only 175km wide, Chile might seem a silly shape for a wine-producing country, certainly when compared with the no-nonsense square shapes of leading producers France and Spain. Yet Chile is envied for its near-perfect vine-growing conditions that have lured legendary European winemaking families such as Torres from Spain and Pontallier and Prats from Bordeaux.

The Chilean climate ranges from desert in the north to Antarctic in the south, offering the full gamut of options in between. Winemaking is confined to a 1,400km section in the middle, around the capital of Santiago. The Central Valley, Chile's most important wine region, comprising Maipo, Rapel, Curicó and Maule, enjoys a Mediterranean climate. The entire length of Chile is cooled, to a greater or lesser extent, by the Antarctic Humboldt Current, and can be irrigated by melting snow from the Andes.

Most remarkable, however, is the fact that Chile is the only wine-producing country in the world to remain immune to the phylloxera aphid, which feeds on and destroys vine roots. As previously mentioned the French industry was almost wiped out by this nasty little blighter in the nineteenth century, and some French producers turned to Chile for replacement rootstocks. And Chile's vineyards have also proved immune to powdery mildew (very nasty). In short, Chile's geography, its climate and its resistance to pests and disease combine to produce some exceptionally healthy fruit.

Chilean wines have surfed a wave of popularity with their fruity, uncomplicated flavours – the vinous equivalent of a packet of fruit pastilles. What's more, they are said to 'overdeliver': a dreadful wine-trade phrase meaning that their quality/price ratio is heavily weighted towards quality. Or, in other words, they're great value for money. While grateful drinkers might ask 'What's not to like?' the wine press has been a little snooty at times about Chile's cheap-and-cheerful reputation.

The accepted view now is that Chilean winemakers are working hard at site selection (matching specific grape varieties with appropriate soils and microclimates) to produce more elegant, characterful wines reflecting their unique growing conditions. They are also becoming 'less heavy-handed' (a handy phrase) in their use of oak – i.e., toning down the toasty, vanilla flavours deriving from barrel-ageing so that they don't dominate. The result is better balance, which is A Good Thing, and you must say so.

Indeed, the word on the street is that Chilean wines are 'growing up' or 'coming of age' – which is a bit rich for an industry that started with the Spanish *conquistadores* in the mid-sixteenth century.

Just as with black fruit pastilles, Chilean red wines seem to be most people's favourites, but the whites are catching up fast. These days, the go-to region for Chardonnay, Sauvignon Blanc and aromatic varieties like Gewürztraminer, Viognier and Riesling is Casablanca. It's a subregion of Aconcagua, Chile's northernmost wine region, and is cooled by Pacific breezes and morning fog – rather like California's northern coast. White wines are also the forte of Bío-Bío, Chile's most southerly major wine region, where the cool conditions have attracted winemakers from Bordeaux and Burgundy.

Cabernet Sauvignon and Merlot are Chile's pre-eminent red grapes, although Syrah and Pinot Noir are putting down roots, too, so to speak. The latter is showing promise in the cool conditions of Casablanca and Bío-Bío.

Amaze your chums with the revelation that much of Chile's 'Merlot' was identified in 1991 as Carmenère, a red grape from Bordeaux which has all but disappeared from that region. There was egg on faces all round for those who had wrongly labelled their Carmenère as Merlot, but some of this egg has since been wiped away with a growing interest for Carmenère in its own right. It makes exceptionally deep-coloured, full-bodied wines, with an unexpected savoury edge, adding oomph to Cabernet Sauvignon or Merlot. For reasons understood only by themselves, some Chileans label their Carmenère as Grande Vidure. Do try to keep up!

Argentina

It is useful for the bluffer to know the signature grape varieties of various wine countries – those varieties that are unique to, or have been adopted by, a place and then presented to the rest of the world as its USP (Unique Selling Point). The USA has Zinfandel, South Africa has Pinotage, New Zealand has Sauvignon Blanc and Australia claims Shiraz (Syrah to everyone else). Of course, France could claim most of the major grape varieties if they hadn't been kidnapped from under their noses and successfully replanted elsewhere. Argentina has not one, but two signature grape varieties: ethereal Torrontés and earthy Malbec (aka 'Beauty and the Beast').

Brooding Malbec, a wild-haired Heathcliff of a grape, was once a lesser member of the Bordeaux family until it was wiped out by the 'famous' frost of 1956, after which they couldn't be bothered to replant it. It is still the principal red grape in Cahors, in southwest France, where it makes what English merchants used to call 'the black wine'. In France it sometimes goes under the names Côt Noir or Auxerrois, but in Argentina both its pride and name have been restored after its shoddy treatment in Bordeaux.

Malbec was first propagated in Argentina in 1852, and it is thought that the cuttings came from Bordeaux, rather than Cahors, which would help to explain the subtle differences between the Argentinian and Cahors versions. In Argentina, where the climate is drier and altitudes higher, the berries are smaller and the tannins riper, making wines more suitable for ageing. It seems that divine providence brought Malbec to Argentina as its chunky structure and ripe damson flavours are the perfect match for beef, another Argentinian speciality.

The best Malbecs come from Mendoza in the eastern foothills of the Andes, but as 80% of Argentinian wine comes from Mendoza, you can be more specific, citing the cooler subregions of Tupungato, the Uco Valley and Upper Mendoza River.

Unlike Malbec, no one has the foggiest idea how the white grape, Torrontés, came to be in Argentina, but this version's worth a punt. In urgent need of sacramental wine, sixteenth-century Jesuits planted the rather bland Criolla Chica variety, though, to be fair, flavour probably wasn't their top priority. Later settlers planted the perfumed Muscat of Alexandria grape, allowing the vines to mingle with Criolla Chica. It is thought that Torrontés is a natural cross of these two varieties, inheriting its sublime aromatic qualities from the Muscat. It might have been named by a homesick Spanish immigrant, because there is a Torrontés grape grown in Galicia in northern Spain, although no connection other than the name has been established. To sound like an authentic *gaucho,* be sure to put the emphasis on the final syllable of *Torron-TÉZ.*

Some of the finest Torrontés comes from the northern high-altitude province of Salta and the cactus-strewn Cafayate Valley that runs through it. Explain that Salta lies on the Tropic of Capricorn, a climate more suited to growing bananas, but the cooling effect of altitude compensates for the subtropical latitude.

At 1,700m above sea level, the vineyards of Cafayate are among the highest – and driest – in the world. Vines are irrigated by meltwater from the Andes, while cool night-time temperatures slow down the ripening process, promoting freshness and crisp acidity in the grapes. Also, there is virtually no vine disease in the dry mountain air. During the day, the sun's rays are particularly intense at this elevation, boosting alcohol levels. It's not unusual for Torrontés from Salta to weigh in at 13.5% or 14% abv – which is deceptively high for such crisp, aromatic whites.

Astound your friends with the fact that the Colomé estate in Payagosta-Salta has the highest vineyards in the world at 3,111m. At high altitude, our sense of taste becomes duller (Exhibit A: airline food), so suggest that Salta's winemakers might inadvertently overcompensate. It would certainly explain the vibrancy and intense fruitiness of their wines.

THE ANTIPODES AND SOUTH AFRICA

Australia

Back in the 1970s, Australian wine was held up as a bit of a joke: 'Kanga Rouge or Wallaby White, anyone?' The industry was forced to eat (drink?) its words in the 1980s when the Aussies started exporting their wines in earnest, making a name for themselves with rich, buttery, oak-laden Chardonnay that was brimming with pineapples and tropical fruit. While European producers had plain old Syrah, you will remember that the Aussies renamed it 'Shiraz', making pumped-up superhero wines – like Syrah, only on steroids.

Aussie wines arrived on our shores like bottled sunshine and a breath of fresh air. Compared with the stifling winemaking regulations of the Old World, Aussie rules meant no rules. They could plant any grape wherever they damn well chose, blending varieties as they pleased to make wines people wanted. And rather than naming these wines after obscure patches of dirt (that *terroir* thing), they labelled their wines by grape variety – and in English. We no longer needed to know that Chablis is made from Chardonnay when we could suddenly buy wines labelled as, you know, 'Chardonnay'.

Thus, the Australians are credited with democratising wine – which is great news for regular wine drinkers, but not so great for bluffers. However, take heart, because things are changing Down Under.

When the Aussies first unleashed their blockbuster wines, they were the darlings of the British wine press for sticking it to The Man (specifically The French). But as soon as we find someone, or something, we love, we want to change them. From the moment Liz Hurley famously bagged legendary cricketer Shane Warne, she wanted him to ditch the thongs and budgie-smugglers for smart-casual or even a suit. Australian wines are undergoing a similar, though less startling, makeover.

Now, you could stick to your guns and say you prefer the unreconstructed 'barbie' wines, but in this instance it's best to go with the flow and join the clamour for subtlety. There's better bluffing to be had.

Opine that you are bored with soulless 'industrial' brands, especially those from the baking dustbowls of Riverina in New South Wales and South Australia's Riverland. These areas are heavily irrigated, and irrigation is a touchy subject in wine circles. Join the French in deriding the practice of watering vines as cheating. Argue that vines need to struggle a bit to make great wines, and for this you need 'dry-grown' vines that produce smaller, more concentrated grapes as opposed to 'hydroponically grown balls of water'.

Today, the Aussies have found out that they've rather overstretched themselves by expanding their vineyards too quickly, only to end up with a surplus of discounted 'critter' brands (so called because they show a marsupial of the month on the label). So where are the Aussies looking for their subtler, more grown-up styles? To cool-climate wine regions where, as you know, slower, steadier ripening produces wines with less alcohol and more acidity – less ripe but with greater elegance and finesse. Of course, as a connoisseur, you approve.

Western Australia's Margaret River and Great Southern coastal regions are cooled by the onshore Fremantle Doctor breeze. The former is noted for its Cabernet Sauvignon and Chardonnay, while the latter is making a name for itself with Pinot Noir, Riesling and Shiraz. These *über*-cool wines do not come cheap, especially those from Margaret River.

In South Australia, look out for zesty Rieslings – here they're more limey than their German counterparts – from the higher-altitude Eden and Clare valleys. The slate at Clare Valley's Polish Hill makes it a particularly favourable site for Riesling. Meanwhile, some of Australia's finest Sauvignon Blanc comes from the cool Adelaide Hills. For extra bluffing points, mention the red terra rossa soil of Padthaway and Coonawarra in the Limestone Coast area, the latter making arguably Australia's best Cabernet Sauvignon, noted for its gazpacho flavours and eucalyptus twang.

In Victoria, near Melbourne, the cool-climate Yarra Valley makes impressive Chardonnay and possibly Australia's best Pinot Noir, a claim that would be contested by the Mornington Peninsula to the south. The cool regions of Beechworth and Geelong also excel with these Burgundian grapes.

So cool it's positively hot, the island of Tasmania also produces top-class Pinot Noir and Chardonnay as well as Pinot Gris and Champagne-method sparkling wines. Riesling and Gewürztraminer are also showing great promise here. Comment that viticulture is relatively new to Tasmania and that quality seems to improve with each vintage as the vines mature.

While cool-climate winemaking and site-selection (matching the best combinations of grape and soil type) are the current watchwords in Australia, you also need to know about two very hot, well-established wine regions. Rutherglen in northeast Victoria, where it really is hot enough to boil a monkey's bum, is deservedly famous for its fortified Liqueur Muscats: rich, sweet, viscous wines with coffee/toffee notes. It is obligatory to refer to them as 'stickies'. And over in South Australia, the Barossa Valley is Australia's biggest quality wine region, its trademark wines being richly concentrated Shiraz, some from vines more than 100 years old.

The Barossa Valley and nearby (relatively speaking, this is Australia we're talking about) McLaren Vale are leading exponents of trendy 'GSM' blends – Grenache, Shiraz and Mourvèdre – whose spiritual home is, of course, the Rhône. It's oh-so-fashionable now to lighten up one's Shiraz with a dash of white Viognier, as they do in Côte-Rôtie. And – whisper it – some Australians have started calling their Shiraz 'Syrah'.

Of course, no good discussion of Aussie wine would be complete without doffing our caps to Penfolds Grange, the first truly great Aussie wine to put the country on the international wine map. Inspired by a trip to Europe in 1950, the late Max Schubert set his sights on creating an Australian red wine to rival Bordeaux's finest, both in terms of quality and ageing potential. One of his great innovations was to mimic the cold conditions of a Bordeaux winery in October by using a simple form of refrigeration to slow the wine's fermentation. Nowadays, of course, temperature-controlled fermentation vats are the norm.

Grange, as you will be aware, is mainly Shiraz with a touch of Cabernet Sauvignon, principally from Barossa, aged in new oak for at least 18 months. It has been officially listed as a 'Heritage Icon' of South Australia, and wine guru Hugh Johnson called it 'the southern hemisphere's only first growth'. As if this weren't recommendation enough, Grange was the only wine deemed good enough for Drew and Libby's flat-warming in *Neighbours*.

And here's a 'Did You Know' to prove your Australian wine credentials: the country's biggest wine brand, Jacob's Creek, is owned by French drinks giant Pernod-Ricard.

South Africa

The line to take with South Africa is that it's the least new of the New World wine countries. Its delectable Muscat-based dessert wines from Constantia date back to the 1650s and enjoyed worldwide renown in the eighteenth century. South African winemakers have tended to emulate the classic European wine styles, valuing structure and restraint over full-on ripeness. They also have an Old World enthusiasm for blending grape varieties, while much of the New World remains focused on single-variety wines.

South Africa's wine lands are concentrated in the Western Cape, spreading north from Cape Town along the Atlantic coast, and east alongside the Indian Ocean. Bluffing potential is good as the major grape varieties are planted throughout in such a diversity of soil types and microclimates that it's hard to claim that any grape is typical of a specific area. But let's try. South Africa possesses a long tradition of cultivating the Cabernet Sauvignon, Chenin Blanc and Semillon grapes, but Rhône varieties are now more fashionable: that's Syrah, Grenache, Cinsault and Mourvèdre among the reds, and Viognier, Grenache Blanc and Roussanne among the whites. Chardonnay and Sauvignon Blanc are also catching on big time. These are sweeping generalisations, but the aspiring bluffer is no stranger to such oversimplifications.

You need to have a passing knowledge of the major wine regions, starting with Stellenbosch. With the greatest concentration of wineries in the Cape, this is the heart of the South African wine industry, making some of the country's finest red wines – something you can attribute to its enviable location. Just to the southeast of Cape Town, Stellenbosch is cooled by breezes from both the Atlantic and Indian oceans. The wineries nestle in valleys and foothills, each with their own microclimate, and these are now being demarcated as individual 'wards' to reflect the region's diversity. Simonsberg-Stellenbosch was the first such ward; Banghoek is one of the newest. The white wines – Chardonnay, Sauvignon Blanc and Chenin Blanc – are now earning as much respect as the reds.

Paarl, just to the north of Stellenbosch and further from the sea, is consequently hotter and making a name for itself with Rhône varieties Syrah and Viognier.

Walker Bay and Elgin are two fancied cool-climate regions in the south with a penchant for Pinot Noir and Chardonnay, the grapes of Burgundy.

Meanwhile, Constantia, a suburb of Cape Town, is responsible for some exhilarating Sauvignon Blanc and Sauvignon/Semillon blends, while the Groot Constantia and Klein Constantia Estates are reviving the region's famous sweet Muscats.

The elephant in the room (appropriate for an African country) is Pinotage. South Africa's very own grape variety divides winemaking opinion as only a grape variety can. It was created in 1925, when Abraham Izak Perold, first professor of viticulture at Stellenbosch University, crossed the rather capricious but delicious

Pinot Noir with Cinsault, the workhorse grape of the Languedoc. Of course, Cinsault is sometimes called Hermitage in South Africa, hence Pinotage.

Good Pinotage bursts on the palate with dark-fruit flavours, a flicker of smoke and a flash of spice with occasional notes of tropical fruit – even banana – reminding us that this grape is unique to Africa. Bad Pinotage exudes rubbery smells and 'acetone' aromas, rather like sniffing glue. Those winemakers who feel they can coax the best out of it hail Pinotage as South Africa's trump card, while those who fear the worst regard it at best as a joker in the pack. Point out that research at the Beyerskloof and Kanonkop wineries, both producers of top-class Pinotage, has led to a greater understanding of this grape, an elimination of off-smells, and some fabulously concentrated wines.

The bluffer should refer to Méthode Cap Classique wines (MCC) as a South African success story. Devised in 1992, MCC is the South African term for classic-method, bottle-fermented sparkling wines, often made solely from Chardonnay. Top South African fizz producers include Boschendal, Pongrácz, Steenberg and Graham Beck.

Avoid referring to modern South African winemakers as 'Cape Crusaders'. Everyone who does it seems to think they're the first to coin the expression. They're not. It's the most overused headline in wine magazines throughout the world.

New Zealand
The next time someone sings the praises of New Zealand Sauvignon Blanc – and it tends to happen frequently

– congratulate them on their fine taste, then pull the rug out from under them with a eulogy to New Zealand Pinot Noir: 'Sure to be the Next Big Thing.' You're not specifying when this might happen. It might never happen, so live for the moment. That's the wonderful thing about punditry: by the time anyone's decided you were right all along, or a complete charlatan, you'll be long gone. The important thing is that you've established yourself as a wine maverick, someone who drinks outside the box.

Anyway, here's the gen on New Zealand Sauvignon Blanc; you don't want to be firing Sauvignon blanks. Inspired by the bone-dry Sauvignon Blancs of Sancerre and Pouilly-Fumé in the Loire, the New Zealand model – picked slightly under-ripe, fermented cool in stainless steel and bottled early – burst onto the scene in the 1980s, like a slap in the face to the Old Country. Often described as grassy or nettley (call it 'herbaceous' for extra points), New Zealand Sauvignon delivers laser-guided gooseberry with tongue-tingling precision.

As you know, New Zealand comprises two major islands, North and South, the latter being the cooler. Which is why you find that the Sauvignons from the North Island tend to have a slightly richer, tropical quality with hints of passion fruit, while those from the South Island have crisper acidity and crunchier gooseberry fruit.

There are few grape variety/regional partnerships as blessed as Sauvignon Blanc and Marlborough, with its temperate maritime climate at the northeastern tip of the South Island. New Zealand's wine industry was originally based entirely on the North Island, in the belief that the South Island was too cool. How times change. The first commercial vineyard wasn't planted in Marlborough until 1973. Now it's the largest wine region in the country, accounting for about half the national vineyard, and Sauvignon Blanc makes up about two-thirds of the national crop.

Even confirmed beer drinkers have heard of New Zealand's iconic Cloudy Bay Sauvignon Blanc, but few know of its stablemate, Te Koko. You, of course, claim to prefer the latter for its richer, creamier style derived from ageing in expensive new oak. Cloudy Bay, you can point out, has minimal oak-ageing.

The go-to regions for New Zealand's supple, red-fruit-scented Pinot Noirs are Martinborough, Waipara and Central Otago, the last of which you can correctly identify as the world's most southerly wine zone.

Other noteworthy regions, both on the North Island, include Hawke's Bay, New Zealand's second-largest wine region with a fine reputation for its Merlot and the other Sauvignon (Cabernet), made in the Bordeaux style; and hot, humid Gisborne, the third-largest wine region and self-proclaimed 'Chardonnay Capital of New Zealand'.

Hawke's Bay's outstanding subregion is the alliterative Gimblett Gravels, worth bringing up if only to sing the praises of its celebrated free-draining soil. Only plumbers and winemakers get so excited about drainage, although it has to be said, grapes do love gravel. It certainly hasn't done Bordeaux's Left Bank any harm, where, you will remember, Graves takes its name from the French word for gravel. Essentially, a steady but moderate water supply restricts vine growth, reducing yields and thus promoting concentration and quality. Slight water stress, as it's known, produces relatively small berries, which is A Good Thing. If anyone asks why, explain patiently that if the berries do not become oversized, then their skin-to-pulp ratios remain high so that the pigments and flavour compounds found largely in the skins are not diluted. Obvious, really. And Gimblett Gravels, by the way, produces particularly good Syrah.

New Zealand's wine continues to enjoy the reputation of a well-known lager brand: 'reassuringly expensive'.

New Zealand produces less than one per cent of the world's wine (less than Romania). However, the laws of supply and demand, bolstered by the generally high quality of New Zealand's output, means NZ wines command the highest average price in the UK: about 40% higher. Consecutive record-breaking harvests in 2008 and 2009 and, some might say, excessive new plantings, have led to the first instances of deep discounting. For the time being, however, New Zealand's wine continues to enjoy the reputation of a well-known lager brand: 'reassuringly expensive'.

B̆

'I drink [Champagne] when I am happy and when I am sad. Sometimes I drink it when I'm alone. When I have company I consider it obligatory. I trifle with it if I'm not hungry and drink it when I am. Otherwise I never touch it – unless I'm thirsty.'

Madame Bollinger

CHAMPAGNE AND OTHER FIZZ

Champagne is for show-offs, making it the bluffer's perfect beverage. Take *sabrage*, for example: the simple technique of opening a bottle with a sabre, made popular when Napoleon's army visited the region. Just hold the bottle facing away from you, then with a backhand movement slide your sabre, blunt-edge forward, along its body towards the neck. As you strike the lip it separates the collar, cork and all, from the neck of the bottle. Huzzah! As Napoleon himself remarked of Champagne, 'In victory you deserve it. In defeat you need it.' And you'll probably never need a glass more than when observing the severed end of your thumb lying in a pool of bubbles and shattered glass. Nonetheless, as a bluffer, you must claim that this is the purist's method of opening. Just don't try it at home.

As you and the late George Best are both aware, Champagne is more than just a drink; it is an expensive lifestyle choice. Assuming you have an attentive audience when drinking the stuff, ram your sybaritic credentials home by quoting the late, great Madame Bollinger: 'I drink [Champagne] when I am happy and when I am sad. Sometimes I drink it when I'm alone. When I have company I consider it obligatory. I trifle with it if I'm not hungry and drink it when I am. Otherwise I never touch it – unless I'm thirsty.'

What a gal!

SERVING CHAMPAGNE

First impressions last, so if you don't have a sabre to hand and you don't want to make a Champagne Charlie of yourself, the best way to open a bottle of fizz is as follows. Once you have stripped away the foil and freed the cork from its wire prison (*la cage*), hold said bottle at an angle of 45 degrees, facing away from eyes and breakable objects. Hold the cork still and gently twist the bottle, tilting the cork sideways slightly, allowing the carbon dioxide to leave with a sigh rather than an undignified bang. Make sure the bottle has been resting in the fridge for at least a couple of hours beforehand (nothing fizzes like warm Champagne) to avoid both injury and the embarrassment of premature ejaculation.

Before you pour, wrap the bottle in a crisp, white damask napkin to conceal the label because a) it is bad form to boast, and b) it might not be Champagne at all, more of which later. Quarter-fill each glass, allow the foam to subside, then top up, leaving sufficient space to 'nose' the heavenly elixir. For added effect, hold the bottle like a sommelier, with your thumb in the indent (the punt) at the base of the bottle. Contrary to popular belief, the punt is not there to short-change you but to further strengthen the thick glass which, you might like to point out, needs to contain the equivalent pressure of a tyre on a London double-decker bus.

And remember, all this pomp and circumstance will be wasted if you serve your fizz in a Champagne saucer or *coupe*. This shallow design allows a) the Champagne to warm up as it is in close contact with your hand, and b) a rapid dissipation of the *mousse* (bubbles). A tall, slender flute glass remedies both a) and b). Note that there are different views on the correct way to fill a flute. Some favour the popular method of pouring it straight into a vertically held glass, so that there is maximum bubble action. But according to recent research in France, pouring Champagne down the side of the glass (at an angle) preserves up to twice as much carbon dioxide (fizz) as pouring it down the middle. This is thought to be due to the gentler pour rate (i.e., reduced speed) at which the Champagne hits the glass. And crucially, you get more in.

HOW CHAMPAGNE IS MADE

When it comes to bluffing about bubbly you need a phrase book. For a start, it's *le* Champagne (the drink) and *la* Champagne (the region), an interesting anomaly you can draw attention to as you admire the fine *mousse* rising in your flute. With Champagne, more than any other type of wine, you need to arm yourself with *les mots justes*.

Champagne is made by the traditional method (*méthode traditionelle*), otherwise known as the classic method (*méthode classique*); for Eurocratic reasons it can no longer be referred to as the Champagne method (*méthode champenoise*). Fundamentally, it's about producing a second fermentation in a bottled wine, which creates the fizz.

The winemaker begins with a palette of still 'base wines' which he mixes into a *cuvée* (blend) in the appropriate house style, in a process called *assemblage*. The region's famous chalky soils and its northerly position – Champagne is France's most northerly appellation (useful bluffing knowledge) – ensure that these base wines have the high levels of acidity that are necessary for quality sparkling-wine production. Explain that it is because Champagne is a blend that it seldom tastes like the still version of, say, Chardonnay plus gas. You might venture that the tooth-stripping acidity of the still wines made in the Coteaux Champenois is the most persuasive argument for making Champagne fizzy.

Once bottled, the blended base wines are enriched with a *liqueur de tirage*, which is a mixture of young wine, sugar and yeast. This provokes the second fermentation called the *prise de mousse*, which is best translated as 'capturing the sparkle'. This usually lasts for about three to five years, during which the bottle is sealed with a temporary crown cap (*bouchon de tirage*). The longer the wine spends in contact with the decomposing yeast, the more it will take on the flavours of dead yeast cells (yummy), a process known as yeast autolysis. 'Ah, a pleasingly autolytic Champagne!' you can exclaim, if it shows the well-bred Champagne flavours of bread, biscuits and brioche.

During this second fermentation period, the bottles are ever-so-slowly tilted from a level position until they are inverted, causing all the sticky, nasty 'lees' (dead and dying yeast cells) to gather in a lump in the neck of the bottle. Traditionally, this process, known as *remuage* (riddling), was helped along by a man in a white coat called a *remueur* (riddler), who tilted each bottle by hand, giving each one a short, sharp twist to encourage the yeast cells down into the neck. A skilled riddler could riddle up to 50,000 bottles a day, but most producers these days do their riddling with automated racks called gyropalettes, developed by the Spanish Cava industry.

Once the yeast cells have finished their downward migration into the neck of the bottle, and the wine is considered to have spent long enough in their company, it is time for *dégorgement* (disgorgement). The bottle necks are plunged into a freezing brine solution, the dead yeast cells turn into an ice plug, the crown cap is removed and the frozen plug bursts forth. The final act is to top up each bottle with a *liqueur d'expédition*, a mixture of still wine and cane sugar, in a process called *dosage*. The larger the dose, the sweeter the Champagne. Each bottle is then sealed with a cork and wire cage.

It should be apparent by now why Champagne is so expensive. So the next time someone complains about the cost, you'll have the ammunition at your fingertips to explain why. It's a risky tactic, as you don't wish to be mistaken for a banker or hedge fund manager, but imply that the whinger in question is one of those people who knows the cost of everything and the value of nothing. You could concede, however, that riddling the bottles, the most cumbersome and costly part of the whole process, is undertaken for purely cosmetic reasons, to prevent the wine from being cloudy – but who wants to drink cloudy Champagne? You wouldn't be able to admire the *mousse*.

The second-best method for making sparkling wines, by some distance, is the *charmat* or 'tank' method, where everything up to the final bottling is done in a pressurised tank. It is much cheaper, quicker and less labour-intensive, but can you taste the love?

The cut-rate method, favoured by cheapskates and meths drinkers, is the injection or 'bicycle-pump' method, as used in the production of soft, fizzy drinks. Carbon dioxide gas is pumped from cylinders into a tank of wine, which is then bottled under pressure. The resulting liquid has lots of big bubbles when poured, but they rapidly fade, leaving the disappointed drinker feeling as flat as his 'fizz'. This method is widely used to make Germany's debilitatingly dry sparkling wine called Sekt. Apparently, when Bismarck was offered a glass by the Kaiser himself, he replied, 'I am sorry, your Majesty. My patriotism stops short of my stomach.' And despite producing industrial volumes of Sekt, Germany is one of the largest importers of Champagne.

So, if you don't see the words *méthode traditionelle* or *méthode classique* (or anglicised derivations thereof), refer to it as 'picnic fizz' and drink it accordingly – like ripping off a plaster. Honourable exceptions can be made for decent Prosecco (*see* page 124).

CHAMPAGNE STYLES

The first distinction to make is between non-vintage Champagne (abbreviated to NV) and the vintage version. Non-vintage (most) Champagne is a blend of wines from several years, whereas vintage fizz is made from the wines of a single year deemed to be exceptionally good. It's not age we pay for, but the perceived quality of that particular vintage – which is why vintage Champagne does not need to be very old in order to command eye-watering prices. In fact, Champagne that is more than about 15 years old turns a darker, toffee-ish colour, takes on a honeyed flavour and loses its sparkle quickly once poured. It's an acquired taste, you can explain, which the French mischievously call *le goût anglais* ('the English taste'), on the grounds that the English, apparently, are into that sort of thing.

To understand the peculiar dry/sweet nomenclature of Champagne you'll need not just a phrase book, but a willing suspension of disbelief. *Brut* is dry, but rarely bone-dry. For that, you need wines labelled *extra brut*, *ultra brut*, *brut sauvage*, *brut zero* or *zero dosage* (no added sugar). Curiously, 'extra dry' denotes a style that is less dry than *brut*. Champagnes described as *sec* are usually quite sweet (off-dry), even though *sec* is French for 'dry'. It's so illogical that you're sure to score bluffing points, first by confusing people (bad cop), then by adopting the role of the kindly expert (good cop) and guiding them through this minefield.

Argue, contentiously, that most people express a preference for dry wines because they think it makes them look sophisticated, yet in blind-tasting situations they frequently prefer off-dry, medium styles. If pressed on this point, explain that this is often the case when focus groups are involved in taste-testing new drinks. Certain cider brands, for example, label their medium ciders as dry for this very reason: to appeal to the faux-sophisticates.

If at a wedding, or any other cake-based celebration, lament the fact that truly sweet Champagne (labelled as *doux* or *riche*) is so hard to come by. It's a much better partner for cakes and desserts, don't you think?

If at a wedding, or any other cake-based celebration, lament the fact that truly sweet Champagne is so hard to come by.

As you know, Champagne can be made from three permitted grape varieties, and each brings something to the party. Chardonnay adds elegance and finesse, Pinot Noir gives body and strength, and Pinot Meunier brings freshness and youth. It is generally considered that Champagne's finest Chardonnay comes from the Côte des Blancs region to the south of Épernay, while its best Pinot Noir comes from the Montagne de Reims, which is as mountainous as Norfolk.

Obviously, Chardonnay is a white grape and the two Pinots are red – or, in Champagne parlance, 'black'. Hence, *blanc de blancs* ('white of whites') denotes a lighter style made solely from Chardonnay, while *blanc de noirs* ('white of blacks') is fuller-bodied Champagne: white, obviously, but made entirely from black grapes. This is achieved by minimising the contact between the freshly pressed juice and the black grape skins, which is where the pigment is found. Most rosé wines are made by controlling this maceration process. Do point out, however, that pink Champagne is one of the very few rosé wines that are made by adding a *soupçon* of red wine to the blend.

Not a lot of people know that.

The most coveted (and certainly most expensive) Champagnes are the *de luxe cuvées*, or *cuvées de prestige*. The mouthwash of oligarchs, footballers, bankers and rappers, these are statement wines for very conspicuous consumption. You could certainly buy two or three bottles of non-vintage Champagne for the price of one *de luxe cuvée*, so do the contents of a deluxe bottle match the bells and whistles of its packaging?

As a discriminating bluffer with a finely tuned palate, you will have to argue that they are worth every penny, and here are the arguments you'll need. *De luxe cuvées* are produced only in limited quantities, made from the best fruit from the top-rated vineyards, using only the juice from the first pressing of the grapes, or the *tête de cuvée* – literally 'head of the blend'. This has fewer of the harsh tannins found in subsequent pressings, so it lends itself to making wines with greater elegance and finesse.

The first *prestige cuvées* were Louis Roederer's Cristal and Moët & Chandon's Dom Pérignon (or 'DP' for those in the know), but now all the leading Champagne houses boast at least one *über*-fizz. Among those to be suitably impressed by are Taittinger's Comtes de Champagne; Krug's Grande Cuvée; Pol Roger's Winston Churchill;

Veuve Clicquot's La Grande Dame; Perrier-Jouët's Belle Époque and Bollinger's RD, which, of course, stands for *récemment dégorgé* ('recently disgorged'). Champagnes that are disgorged (removed from their lees) at the last moment before going to market seem to retain their freshness and fruity expression regardless of their age.

According to the company, Cristal was created by Louis Roederer in 1876 for Tsar Alexander II, who allegedly insisted on the now-iconic clear glass bottle so he could see what he was drinking (uneasy lies the head that wears a crown, and all that). The hip-hop community embraced Cristal so everyone else could see what they were drinking, but the rappers have since dropped Cristal like a hot *pomme de terre*.

Offence was taken at comments, which were deemed disrespectful, from Roederer's headquarters, allegedly suggesting the association with hip-hop was 'unwelcome' (subsequently denied). This is pretty rich, coming from a culture that referred to Cristal as 'Crissy' and drank it from the bottle through a straw. You might know your RD from your DP, but if you want to get down with the kids, you need to know that rappers soon moved on to Armand de Brignac (with its nice, understated gold bottle).

GROWING TO LIKE YOU

The Champagne business is dominated by the illustrious houses known as *les grandes marques*, most of which are based in Épernay and Reims (which you must pronounce as *Ranz*, never *Reems*). You, however, are aware that this swanky club owns only a small percentage of the region's vineyards and that they buy in most of their grapes from around 15,000 small farmers.

Because you have your finger on the pulse, you also know that one of the most important recent developments in Champagne is that increasing numbers of these humble growers are making and selling their own Champagne. These are known, not surprisingly, as growers' Champagnes, and they now account for about a quarter of Champagne sales. Importantly, it is perfectly acceptable – almost *de rigueur* – to rate them as more 'characterful' than the major brands. You can identify the wines of these crazy mavericks by spotting the initials 'RM' on the label. Explain that this stands for *récoltants-manipulants* (growers who make their own wines), as opposed to 'NM', which stands for *négociants-manipulants* (who produce Champagne from purchased grapes, like *les grandes marques*).

As for the relatively recent (2008) decision simply to extend the boundaries of the Champagne region, you have mixed views. Say that it rather makes a mockery of the *appellation controlée* system, which sets in stone which wines can be made on which hallowed ground, and that it's a cynical attempt to meet the enormous demand from Chinese and Russian oligarchs. Then again, if it means more fizz to go round, who's complaining?

OTHER FIZZ: OLD WORLD

Champagne comes only from the Champagne region. Refer to any other sparkling wine as 'Champagne' and you might as well hand in your bluffer's badge and go home now. Other sparkling wines exist, and many of them are made by the same traditional method. The line you take should depend on the health of your bank account. If you can afford to buy Champagne regularly you should say that nothing else comes close. If you operate on a more frugal fizz budget, you could say that the best sparkling alternatives are a match, certainly for non-vintage Champagne, and at a fraction of the price. It's called fancy footwork and politicians do it all the time.

Crémant

If you're buying French bubbly on a budget, look out for *crémant* wines. The term refers to dry sparkling wines made by the traditional method anywhere outside Champagne. Helpfully suggest Crémant de Die from the northern Rhône, made mainly from the light Clairette grape variety; Crémant de Loire, generally made from Chenin Blanc; Crémant de Bordeaux, usually Sémillon or Sauvignon Blanc; Crémant d'Alsace, usually Pinot Blanc, sometimes Chardonnay; the Languedoc's Crémant de Limoux, made from Chardonnay and Chenin Blanc; and Crémant de Bourgogne (Burgundy), which even uses two of the Champagne grape varieties, Chardonnay and Pinot Noir. If you conceal the label beneath a napkin as you pour, you might even be able to pass some of these off as 'the real thing'. The same can be said of the best English sparklers, which regularly outscore Champagne in blind tastings (*see* page 87).

Cava

Spanish Cava, you can explain, is made by the traditional Champagne method but mainly from the Parellada,

Macabeo and Xarel-lo grape varieties. Chardonnay is entering the frame these days, with a few Cavas being made exclusively from this grape. Pinot Noir, meanwhile, is permitted in the increasingly popular pink Cava.

Made throughout Spain, but mainly in the Penedès area of Catalonia, Cava is dominated by two giant producers; Freixenet (pronounced *FRECH-e-nett*), best known for its Cordon Negro in the frosted black bottle, and Codorníu, which favours the use of non-indigenous grapes. Enthuse about the Anna de Codorníu brand, especially the Brut Rosé, which is a blend of mostly Pinot Noir with some Chardonnay. Impress your mates with the fascinating fact that Codorníu is the world's biggest producer of traditional-method sparkling wines – bigger than any of the Champagne producers.

Freixenet and Codorníu are the Ford and General Motors of Cava, so you will score serious points for name-dropping the following upmarket producers: Gramona, Marqués de Monistrol, Parxet, Castillo Perelada, Juvé & Camps, Segura Viudas (owned by Freixenet) and Raïmat (owned by Codorníu, and maker of a rare 100% Chardonnay Cava). Explain how you enjoyed necking these *bijoux* brands on Las Ramblas in Barcelona, but express your frustration at how hard they are to find at home.

Should anyone get sniffy about Cava, tell them it's time to reconsider their prejudice: lower yields and longer bottle-ageing are steadily improving quality. Suggest they might have had a bottle that was past its best, because Cava is definitely at its best when young and fruity.

Prosecco

Italian Prosecco is mostly made by the *charmat* method, where the second fermentation takes place in a large tank, but don't let this put you off. Produced mainly in Valdobbiadene-Conegliano to the north of Venice, Prosecco is the Italian *aperitivo* of choice. Indeed, a trendsetter such as yourself will know that Prosecco sales have gone through the roof in recent years as more of us succumb to its uncomplicated charms. You will also be aware that not all Prosecco is effervescent. It can be made into a very dull still wine, but when fizzed up, which is the norm, it positively sparkles (and sparkles positively).

Correct anyone who tells you that 'Prosecco' is the name of both the grape variety and the wine it produces. Inform them as patronisingly as possible that, yes, this was the case until very recently (2009) but the grape has now been renamed 'Glera'. The thinking behind this? Now that Prosecco is the name of the wine only, anything made with the same grape but outside the strictly designated areas of Veneto and Friuli must call itself Glera. And would *you* drink something that sounds like a window-cleaning product?

Compared to Champagne, Prosecco is both cheap and cheerful. It's light and fresh, occasionally quite aromatic, with an apple-and-pear fruitiness. Off-dry is the default style, with truly dry quite scarce. Connoisseurs like you know that *frizzante* on the label means semi-sparkling, while *spumante* is full-on, head-banging fizzy. Like Cava, any Prosecco more than two years old should be treated with extreme caution.

Brands to get excited about include Bisol, Carpene-Malvolti, Adami, Ruggeri, Zardetto, Le Colture and Nino Franco.

Would *you* drink something that sounds like a window-cleaning product?

Prosecco's fruity qualities are neatly demonstrated in the classic Bellini cocktail. Never be so gauche as to use Champagne for this, because its yeasty, biscuity – hey, 'autolytic' – qualities are rather overpowering in this light, fruity context. Inform your rapt audience that the Bellini was created between the wars by Giuseppe Cipriani in Venice's legendary Harry's Bar.

A proper Bellini comprises one-third white peach purée topped up with two-thirds Prosecco, stirred and garnished with a slice of peach. It is named, of course, after the Venetian painter Giovanni Bellini, whose paintings were famous for their sumptuous colours; the original recipe included a dash of raspberry or cherry juice for a rosy-pink glow.

As delicious as they are, Bellinis are pretty much old hat these days. The up-to-the-minute bluffer prefers his Prosecco mixed with Aperol (sort of Campari Lite), to make an Aperol Spritz. This fruity, off-dry, pink *aperitivo* is all the rage in northern Italy, where some 300,000 are sipped every day in Veneto alone, according to the good people at Aperol. Mix two parts Aperol with three parts

Prosecco (dash of soda optional) for a very sophisticated sharpener.

Finally, don't forget (again) to look for English fizz and claim with some justification that it performs consistently well in blind tastings.

OTHER FIZZ: NEW WORLD

Of course, one thing the New World has that Champagne hasn't is reliable ripening of its grapes, year in, year out, owing to the warmer climates. But this can be a double-edged sword. Even the coolest New World climates are not as cool as Champagne's, so the growers have to strike a fine balance between picking their grapes slightly early to preserve much-needed acidity, but risking unripe, 'green' flavours in the finished wines; or picking later to achieve more ripeness but risking overly alcoholic wines with insufficient acidity. Thus, even more than with still-wine production, cool-climate regions are the Holy Grail for sparkling winemaking in the New World.

So which New World sparklers can the bluffer uncork with confidence amongst his peers? There are plenty that fit the bill, with many of the finest examples produced in outposts of the Champagne empire, many in joint ventures with local producers.

The most promising regions in Australia are the relatively cool-climate Yarra Valley in Victoria and the even cooler Tasmania, especially in its subregions of the Tamar Valley and Pipers River. In fact, so highly rated are the sparkling wines of Tasmania that many Australian fizz producers ship in Tasmanian base wines to lift the acidity in their blends. Tasmanian names to look out for include Pipers Brook, Bay of Fires and Jansz, which originally started as a joint venture with Champagne house Louis Roederer.

On the mainland, Moët & Chandon was the first Champagne house to take the plunge, establishing Domaine Chandon in the Yarra Valley in 1987. Its wines are sold under the highly rated Green Point label in the UK. Also worthy of the bluffer's attention are the sparkling wines of Croser in Petaluma in the Adelaide Hills, and Salinger from Seppelt in the Barossa Valley.

Expect plenty of 'ooohs' and 'aaahs' if you whip out a bottle of red sparkling Shiraz. Typically semi-sweet with relatively high alcohol, this unique sparkling style originated in Victoria in the nineteenth century, when it was called 'sparkling Burgundy', and it experienced a resurgence in the 1980s. A brasher, more 1980s-style of wine would be hard to find. The best producers use the traditional method, and these include Langmeil in Victoria's Barossa Valley, which claims to have the oldest Shiraz vines in the world, planted in 1843. You are, of course, by now familiar with the fact that most of Europe's vineyards were wiped out by the phylloxera bug in the late nineteenth century.

Across the southern ocean, New Zealand's altogether cooler climate is generally better equipped to provide the prized acidity for sparkling winemaking. On the South Island, Marlborough has been the source of excellent fizz since the early 1980s. You can crack open any sparkling wine from the Nautilus brand, Cloudy Bay's

Pelorus and Deutz Marlborough Cuvée (yes, Deutz, as in the Champagne house), safe in the knowledge that they will impress. Likewise, you'll be secure enough in opening the wines of Lindauer, although these are made in Auckland on the North Island and not all of them are bottle-fermented in the traditional manner. The reasonably priced Lindauer Brut and top *cuvée* Lindauer Grandeur are, however, made in the time-honoured way and are well worth a pop.

The hot new style in New Zealand fizz is sparkling Sauvignon Blanc – well, it had to happen, didn't it? But the jury is still out on whether this crisp, fresh and undemanding style is merely a convenient vehicle for shifting surplus Sauvignon.

In California, the regions to pay special attention to are Anderson Valley in northern Mendocino, Russian River Valley in Sonoma County, and Carneros, which straddles the southern ends of Sonoma and Napa. After extensive research, Louis Roederer opted for Anderson Valley for its Roederer Estate winery. Its rosé is particularly good.

Sparkling wines were made in California as far back as the 1890s, but again, Moët & Chandon was the first Champagne house to take the plunge, setting up the Domaine Chandon winery in Napa in 1973. Champagne Mumm also opted for Napa (Mumm Napa Valley); Champagne Deutz went for Santa Barbara (Maison Deutz); Piper-Heidsieck chose Sonoma (Piper-Sonoma); and Taittinger was seduced by Carneros (Domaine Carneros). Meanwhile, Schramsberg in the Napa Valley remains one of the finest American fizzes.

In 1992, South Africans coined the phrase 'Méthode Cap Classique' (MCC) to describe bottle-fermented sparkling wines from the Cape. Top South African fizz producers include Pongrácz, of Hungarian descent, in Stellenbosch; Steenberg in Constantia; Graham Beck in Stellenbosch and Robertson; Krone in the Tulbagh Valley; and Boschendal and Haute Cabrière, both in Franschhoek, which means the 'French corner'. Haute Cabrière's brand, Pierre Jourdan, is named after the first Huguenot farmer to settle in the area.

Those Frenchies get everywhere.

Even if you find the peculiar salty tang of dry fino Sherry an acquired taste, you must at least pretend you have acquired it if you wish to appear sophisticated.

FORTIFIED WINE

SHERRY

Proper wine buffs wear their appreciation of Sherry as a badge of connoisseurship, so even if you find the peculiar salty tang of dry fino Sherry an acquired taste, you must at least pretend you have acquired it if you wish to appear sophisticated. Of course, you must serve it chilled, perhaps with a dish of salted almonds or slivers of Ibérico ham, sliced from the bone.

You need to know that 'Sherry' is an anglicisation of Jerez, the city in Andalucía at the heart of Sherry production. You will pronounce it *herr-ETH* because you are a frequent visitor and you know these things. Most Sherry is made from the Palomino grape variety, grown on chalky *albariza* soil for which the region is famous. Quip that your favourite Sherry styles are as bone-dry as the soil.

All types of Sherry are aged for at least three years and are made in the *solera* system. Say that this system is P2C2E (a Process too Complicated to Explain) but you will manfully (or womanfully) have a go. Essentially, the *bodega* (or cellar) contains rows of barrels holding Sherries of different ages. About a third of the contents of the oldest barrels are bottled. This is topped up with wine from the second-oldest barrels, which are topped up with wine from the next-oldest barrels, and so on. The youngest barrels contain the current vintage, and there must be a minimum of three sets of barrels. Thus, young and old wines are blended together and the blend is constantly refreshed. It's a bit like playing with Russian dolls, only with barrels.

There are two principal types of Sherry: pale, dry styles such as fino and manzanilla, which age under a thin film of natural yeast called *flor* that grows on the surface of the wine; and dark, dry oloroso, which is made without *flor*. These are the starting points for all Sherry styles.

Wines destined to become fino/manzanilla are fortified sparingly to encourage the growth of *flor*. In fact, the annual addition of younger wines from the *solera* system feeds the *flor*, helping to maintain an even layer. The pleasingly alliterative fine film of *flor* protects the maturing wines from contact with the air, which gives them their typically sharp, pungent tang – a quality you can describe as *rancio,* which is perfectly polite in wine circles even though it basically means 'rancid'. As you've probably guessed by now, fino and manzanilla are essentially the same, only manzanilla is made in the comparatively cool seaside conditions of Sanlúcar de Barrameda, where the *flor* grows thicker, giving the wines an even more pronounced salty tang.

Proper dry amontillado Sherry is fino/manzanilla that has been left to age after the *flor* has died, which takes about five years, meaning it completes its ageing process in contact with the air. You must describe true amontillado as 'nutty'; that's the rule. 'Improper' amontillado is a commercial, medium-sweet concoction whereby the dry Sherry is sweetened with *mistela,* a blend of grape juice and alcohol. Obviously, you prefer the proper version.

As mentioned, oloroso is matured without any *flor*, meaning it is in contact with air throughout the entire maturation process, which has the effect of darkening it. Oloroso Sherry is fuller-bodied than fino/manzanilla but remains dry. It tends to be 'nutty' like amontillado, but you can add the required 'raisiny' adjective. Wines earmarked for oloroso are more strongly fortified to prevent the development of *flor*. Sometimes oloroso is sweetened to become cream Sherry.

So, what's Palo Cortado? In her excellent *Oxford Companion to Wine,* Jancis Robinson OBE MW (Master of Wine) calls it 'a naturally resulting intermediate type and style between amontillado and oloroso'. And if that's good enough for Ms Robinson, it's good enough for the rest of us. All you really need to know is that nutty, dry Palo Cortado ('pale cut') is the rarest type of Sherry, made when *flor* doesn't occur, and it is aged for decades. Consequently, should you find yourself in the presence of Palo Cortado you must roll on your back and wave your legs in the air.

This leaves thick, black, syrupy Pedro Ximénez Sherry, made from the sun-dried Pedro Ximénez grape.

Call it simply 'PX' for maximum bluffing points. Not only are you allowed to pour this over vanilla ice cream with a handful of raisins, it is actively encouraged by certain wine writers. Do as they do, then – and bask in their reflected glory.

Port can really make your brain hurt, both figuratively and literally with the almighty hangovers it produces.

PORT

Port and Sherry are both fortified wines, but that is where the similarities end. Sherry is made (mostly) from a single white grape, Palomino, while Port is a blend of big, butch red grapes like Touriga Nacional, Touriga Franca, Tinta Roriz, Tinta Cão and Tinta Barroca. But the biggest difference – the reason why Sherry is crisp and dry while Port is sweet – has to do with *when* these wines are fortified with grape spirit. Sherry is fortified *after* the wine has finished fermenting, after all the sugar in the grape juice has been consumed by yeast. With Port, however, grape spirit is added *before* the wine has finished fermenting, before all the grape sugars have been consumed by yeast. The addition of grape spirit during fermentation causes the fermentation to stop, leaving plenty of sweet, unfermented grape sugar in the wine. Refer to this as 'residual' sugar.

The British were instrumental in creating the Port style in the seventeenth century. Trade wars with France meant that the Brits had to find an alternative source of wine, and Portugal, a trusted ally, was happy to oblige. Unfortunately, the wines spoiled on their voyage to Blighty unless they were fortified with brandy. British wine merchants colonised the Douro Valley, where Port is made, and have stayed there ever since. Incidentally, the Douro was established as a formally recognised wine region ('demarcated') in 1756, predating the French *appellation contrôlée* system.

Now, if you thought Sherry was complicated, Port can really make your brain hurt, both figuratively and literally with the almighty hangovers it produces (if consumed to excess). The big deal with Port is whether it's wood-aged (in a barrel) or bottle-aged; wood-aged is generally lighter in colour, spicier and nuttier, than the deeply coloured, overtly fruity, bottle-aged styles. Wine buffs also get very excited about whether a Port is filtered or unfiltered, the latter being dense with residual solids (dead yeast cells, etc.) that give flavour and body to the wine and help it to improve with age. When the gunk sinks to the bottom of the bottle, the wine is said to have 'thrown a deposit', which requires the rigmarole of decanting it (*see* page 18) to separate it from the wine.

The complexity of the various Port classifications makes Sherry's *solera* system look like child's play. It is not helped by what seems to be a competition among Port producers to see who can mention the word 'vintage' the most times on a label, even if the wine behind the label has as much to do with vintage Port as it does with vintage cars and vintage fashion. But if you want to bluff your way through Port, you need to be familiar with some of the principal styles.

Proper vintage Port is the poshest Port of all, with prices to match. Made from only the finest grapes from the best vineyards, it accounts for no more than one per cent of Port production. Dark-purple, heavily tannic, intensely rich and fruity, it can take 20 years before it starts to reach its best. Because vintage Port takes so long to 'come round', it was a traditional christening present for boys, as child and wine would come of age at roughly the same time. The correct amount to give was a barrel, or 'pipe', containing about 50-dozen bottles.

Explain that vintage Port is a blend of wines from a single year, considered to be exceptional and officially 'declared' as such. Comment that this happens, on average, about three times per decade and that the decision to declare is a matter left up to the individual producers. Vintage Port is a bottle-aged style, bottled unfiltered after spending two or three years in wood, then left to mature. Naturally, it throws a deposit, so it requires decanting.

The other bottle-aged styles are single-*quinta* vintage and crusted Port. Single-*quinta* vintage Port is made in the same way as vintage Port, but is the produce of an individual *quinta* or estate. These same wines are blended together to make vintage Port in officially declared years, but are released as single-*quinta* Ports in years considered to be pretty good but not quite up to vintage standards.

Like the single-*quinta* wines, crusted Port is designed to appeal to vintage Port enthusiasts but without the hefty price tag. Crusted Port is a blend of wines from a number of years, bottled young with little or no filtration, after three or four years in cask. It is so called because of the sediment or 'crust' it throws in the bottle.

Which brings us, mercifully, to the wood-aged Ports. Pour yourself a drink and we'll get through this together. Wood-aged Ports do their ageing in barrels, or cement tanks, and are bottled – usually filtered – when they're ready to drink.

The style known as aged tawny is matured in cask for at least six years, and named after its amber-brown, tawny hue. Sometimes it is labelled as 10, 20, 30 or 40 years old, but these are approximations, as tawny Port is blended from the wines of several years. Comment that the 30- and 40-year-old wines aren't always worth the premium they command over the perfectly delicious 10- and 20-year-olds. Tawny's nutty, fig-like flavours are best enjoyed slightly chilled, making it the Port producer's everyday tipple of choice. *Colheita* Port is tawny Port from a single vintage, matured in cask for at least seven years, often longer. It is potentially the finest of the aged tawnies.

Late-bottled vintage Port (abbreviated to LBV) is wine from a single year, matured in cask for four to six years. That sounds straightforward enough, but, guess what, there are two styles of LBV. There is traditional LBV, which is bottled unfiltered, and the much more common basic LBV, which is filtered.

As you probably know by now, the unfiltered traditional LBV will require decanting and will continue to improve in the bottle for a few years. Made in good but undeclared years, it is a dark, full-bodied Port, offering a decent alternative to full-blown vintage Port at a fraction of the cost. Bog-standard LBV, because it is filtered, offers a lighter, less intense experience and is unlikely to improve once bottled. The trade-off is that it has no sediment, so doesn't need decanting. Naturally, you prefer traditional LBV.

Ruby Port is the cheap-and-cheerful wood-aged option, aged in bulk for one to three years, then filtered and bottled while still young and fiery with a deep-ruby colour. Best consumed with lemonade.

By the time we reach vintage character, sometimes known as vintage reserve, we can justifiably run away screaming, 'Vintage, schmintage!' (Which is quite hard to say.) In theory, these are premium rubies, aged in bulk, usually in wood, for up to five years before being bottled, filtered. These are not even wines from a single year, as the word 'vintage' would imply. Many Port shippers, possibly feeling embarrassed, have removed this ridiculous phrase from their labels, replacing it with their own brand names instead.

White Port does exist, made from white grapes like Moscatel, but as Ernest Cockburn (a leading authority on these matters) once remarked, 'The first duty of Port is to be red.' Relatively few taste dry and nutty from wood-ageing. Most white Port is rather sweet and best served, as they do in the Douro, with tonic water and a slice of lemon.

MADEIRA

Madeira is the only wine to be 'boiled' – deliberately. The process is called the *estufa* system and involves heating the wine to 120°F (49°C) for a considerable length of time, which is what gives it a distinctive burnt flavour. 'And all this,' you can say knowingly, 'is to simulate what happened to Madeira when it was used as ballast on sailing ships for the long voyages to Africa and the Indies and accidentally got cooked *en route* as it crossed and re-crossed the equator.'

Madeira is also made from odd grape varieties – Sercial, Verdelho, Bual and Malmsey – or it's supposed to be. There is a rumour (and here the bluffer can wink knowingly) that these have been supplanted by a much less noble grape called Tinta Negra Mole.

Only claim to be an expert as a last resort and if you are wearing a suit. For some reason waiters do not believe that casually dressed people can know anything about wine.

WINING AND DINING

It is important to remember that restaurants make most of their profits from wine, and it is not uncommon to find mark-ups of 300–400%. The situation is even worse in France, where greedy restaurateurs push the price of ordinary wine out of the reach of those who need it most. But a mark-up of 200% is considered almost a minimum anywhere, and that can hardly be described as reasonable.

Some restaurants get away with scandalous prices: people fork out at least double the average high-street price for the most basic plonk in unexceptional brasseries without demur. This is a depressing reality. Bear in mind that this wine, often of the most dubious provenance, probably cost the producer the equivalent of a box of matches to make, and even with shipping and duty and a reasonable profit margin for the grower and merchant, it can hardly cost the restaurant more than the price of a cheap cigar.

When going to a licensed restaurant, you must also

be aware that you are letting yourself in for an elaborate ritual. Wine waiters are taught to go through various motions, handing the wine list to the most important-looking person, pouring out a little for him (and it usually is him) to taste, but they are rarely taught the purpose of these motions.

For this reason – and because most people are so extraordinarily deferential – wine waiters do not take at all kindly to having their wines sent back. The few simple rules below may help you to hold your own:

1. If you are going to reject the wine, you need to do so immediately after the waiter has given you a small amount to taste. If you delay and start drinking, the waiter will understandably assume that either you are unsure of your ground, or the wine is drinkable.

2. Be polite but firm. Any trace of hesitancy plays right into the hands of the waiter, who invariably assumes the customer is stupid, wrong or just trying it on.

3. Only claim to be an expert as a last resort and if you are wearing a suit. For some reason waiters do not believe that casually dressed people can know anything about wine.

Of course, tactics of this kind really shouldn't be necessary. They can ruin a perfectly planned romantic evening. On the other hand, it may also be a good test. After all, a partner who will not allow you to challenge a wine waiter may not be prepared to give you much leeway in other areas. Best to find this out now, when your only consequence is paying for overpriced plonk.

'WAITER, THIS WINE IS CORKED'

It is widely believed that, in order to qualify as a real wine expert, you need to be able to tell instantly whether or not a wine is corked. In fact, no wine term is attended by so much confusion. Some people, in their innocence, believe that a corked wine has bits of cork floating around in it; this is not the case. Bits of cork, however unsightly, in no way affect the taste of wine. If they did, every bottle would be corked, since the wine inside is constantly in contact with the cork.

Some quite knowledgeable people say that a corked wine 'tastes of' cork. But seeing as not many of us chew cork for fun, it is easier to recognise as wine that smells musty and dank, like a house with rising damp, or more or less completely flat (i.e., tasteless). You might take the line that the word 'corked' is strictly meaningless and that it is much more honest to use the term 'off' – if for no other reason than that it is anathema to the wine expert. But if you want to shine, explain that the problem is caused by '2,4,6 TCA': i.e., trichloroanisole – a chemical compound that sometimes occurs when corks are bleached before washing.

There are various kinds of 'off-ness'. Apart from the dank, musty odour, there is oxidation. This is what happens when wine is exposed to the atmosphere. It ends up going brown and smelling a bit like toffee.

With some wines, especially Sherry and Madeira, this is actually considered desirable, and the word 'maderised' (i.e., tasting like Madeira) is a good term to master and employ when faced with any wine that's tired, old or has been sitting around for far too long. It could also apply to some people, come to that.

It is important to remember that there is no such thing as an airtight screwcapped wine which is 'screwed' (see page 17).

WINE AND FOOD

Most wine, of course, cries out to be drunk with food. It is obvious that a fine red Burgundy or California Cabernet was not made to be drunk on its own. The same is true of the more alcoholic white wines like white Burgundy or Sauternes. But some lighter wines, mainly white but occasionally red, are actually more suited for unaccompanied consumption.

The Bach solo violin *partitas* of the wine world are the great Rieslings of the Mosel-Saar-Ruwer. The Maximin Grünhaus wines of von Schubert, for instance, are too delicate and fine to have intercourse with any food. The dry Muscats of Alsace are best drunk as an apéritif.

As to the great vexed issue of which wine goes with which food, bluffers should not feel intimidated. The golden rule is that there are no golden rules. The classic axiom is that only white wine can be served with fish. It has to be admitted that most fish dishes are best accompanied by white wines, from Muscadet with shellfish to Meursault with, say, sole in a rich, creamy sauce. But the Basque dish of salt cod and ratatouille is so strongly flavoured that it needs a red wine to cope with it, and some dark-fleshed fish, like salmon and fresh tuna, are particularly well suited to a fairly light red. You might try some really outrageous combinations for fun: Châteauneuf with oysters, perhaps, or Coquilles St-Jacques au Zinfandel. Or at least claim to have tried them.

There is also a belief that most cheeses, including the white-rinded ones like Brie and Camembert, are a particularly suitable accompaniment to the finest Bordeaux (claret). This is not true. White-rinded cheeses completely alter the character of fine red wines, making them taste strangely sweet. Hence the old wine trade adage, 'Buy on an apple, sell on cheese', but this only works with cheaper wines. Château Lafite with Brie is nothing like its true self and might just as well be Beaujolais.

Even Cheddar can be too strong and pungent for claret. The only cheeses that go really well with fine red wine are very hard, subtly flavoured ones, like the Italian pecorino and the fine Manchego cheeses from Spain. The traditional combination of Port and Stilton, on the other hand, can be accorded your unqualified respect.

OVERINDULGENCE: HEALTH AND HANGOVERS

The old bluffing line on this used to consist of a fruity chuckle and a suggestion that wine had much in common with sex: the more the merrier, within reason (and reason can be stretched to the limit in these matters). Today, should you wish to champion the health benefits of regular wine consumption, you can support your claim with a beguiling array of scientific arguments endorsed by leading clinicians.

Your opening gambit is 'the French paradox': the French, infuriatingly, have a relatively low incidence of coronary heart disease despite having a diet that is rich in saturated fats (cheese, pâté, duck confit, etc). Then you produce the trump card: far from being serendipitous coincidence, moderate consumption of red wine has been proved to reduce incidence of heart disease by up to 50%. The key benefit is that red wine helps mop up the body's 'free radicals', the sweet-sounding but dangerous chemicals liable to cause allergic reactions.

This French research was not only backed by Danish scientists in 1995, but also by the *Journal of the American Geriatrics Society*, which reported that up to three glasses of wine a day may reduce the risk of developing Alzheimer's. So where you used to drink to forget, you can now drink to remember.

You can then reel out a string of other claims: wine can flush out kidney stones, help ease rheumatoid arthritis, contains a natural antidote to cancer, counters salmonella and E coli and can cure diarrhoea more effectively than regular pills and potions.

Despite all the above, wine does still have an annoying tendency to cause hangovers. Of course, these might have something to do with alcohol, but the bluffer can suggest that the supposedly hangover-inducing qualities of many red wines are in fact caused by histamines, and that these can be counteracted by the simple method (pioneered by Michael Broadbent, the great English wine expert) of taking antihistamine tablets.

Ƀ

There's no point in pretending that you know everything about wine – nobody does. But if you've got this far and you've absorbed at least a modicum of the information and advice contained within these pages, then you will almost certainly know more than 99% of the rest of the human race about what wine is, how it is made, where it is made, how it is served, and how it is drunk.

What you now do with this information is up to you, but here's a suggestion: be confident about your new-found knowledge, see how far it takes you, but above all, have fun using it. And bear in mind that the only bluffing skill that really matters is the ability to choose your moment carefully and keep your mouth shut the rest of the time. That's easy enough to do when it's full of fermented grape juice.

GLOSSARY

Appellation Designated area of wine production that is protected by elaborate laws (which are either ignored or irrelevant).

AC *Appellation contrôlée.* Applies to French wines from designated regions of which certain standards are demanded. Doesn't necessarily mean they're any good.

Austere A wine that has roughly the same effect on your palate as hard water on copper pipes.

Barrique A fancy name for a barrel, specifically a standard Bordeaux barrel holding 225 litres.

Biodynamic wine 'Hippy' wine made according to biodynamic principles. Vines are treated with infusions of mineral, animal and plant materials according to cosmic forces and the movement of the planets. Really.

Botrytis A friendly fungus essential in producing sweet

wines like Sauternes. Infected berries shrivel and dry on the vine, concentrating natural sugar. Known as 'noble rot'.

Bottle-sick A temporary condition that affects wines immediately after bottling. Not the condition that affects people after drinking too many bottles.

Cap(sule) Metal or plastic deterrent that covers the cork. Metal ones are fine, so long as they are made of lead, but there is no known aid for the tough plastic ones.

Cépage French for grape variety.

Chaptalisation French for the practice of adding sugar to the must or unfermented grape juice. It was named after a chap called Jean-Antoine Chaptal who invented it in the eighteenth century. The French have shrewdly decided that it sounds better than 'the practice of adding sugar'.

Château a) In France, a castle or stately home; b) in Bordeaux, any building, outhouse, shed in which or near which wine is made or stored.

Château-**bottled** Wine bottled in the aforementioned building, outhouse, shed, etc.

Climat A few rows of vines in Burgundy.

Commune French for 'parish'.

Cru French for 'growth', which is best translated as 'vineyard'. The best French wines like to call themselves *grands crus* ('great growths'), *premiers crus* ('first growths'), *'premiers grands crus'* (first great growths), etc.

Cuvée French word for 'a blend'.

DO *Denominación de origen.* Much the same as the French AC, only Spanish.

DOC *Denominazione di origine controllata.* Much the same as the Spanish DO, only Italian.

Extract That which makes a wine taste nice and isn't alcohol, acidity, fruit or sugar.

Garagiste Not someone who repairs your car, or plays loud music, but a new-wave Bordeaux producer who makes very expensive boutique wine in his or her garage. Examples are *châteaux* Valandraud and Le Pin.

Gouleyant Excellent French word meaning 'gulpable'.

Great Any wine or vintage that is better than average.

Lees Old English word for 'gunk' (sediment) that settles at the bottom of a container such as a fermentation vessel. In a wine context, this gunk comprises grape seeds, stems, bits of skin and dead yeast cells. Wines like Muscadet are sometimes matured *sur lie* in an attempt to add body and flavour.

Marc (Pronounced *Maaarrh*) A kind of brandy made by distilling grape skins, pips, etc. Known in Italy as grappa.

Malolactic fermentation A softening process sometimes induced after alcoholic fermentation to convert harsh malic acid into softer lactic (milky) acid.

Moelleux French for 'quite sweet'. Difficult word to pronounce even before drinking some.

MOG American for *M*atter *O*ther than *G*rapes: 'I see a little MOG has crept in here.'

Négociant French for a wine merchant who buys, blends and bottles his own wines.

Oechsle German scale of measuring the ripeness of grapes. To talk about Oechsle numbers for wines ('Ah yes, 117° Oechsle – phenomenal') is the equivalent of using Köchel numbers for Mozart's works.

Oenologist The wine professional's professional.

Oidium Nasty little word for a nasty little fungus which shrivels grapes and turns them grey, in a bad way. Not like botrytis, the friendly fungus.

Ordinaire Undistinguished.

Palate Soft plate at the back of the mouth which is supposed to be an organ of taste. The palate hasn't got very much to do with taste at all, as it happens. People with good palates are supposed to be skilled tasters. In fact, a good palate probably just helps you to speak distinctly.

Parker, Robert Jr American lawyer who had the idea of awarding wine scores out of 100. Like most American students, none gets below 60, and many score in the 90s. Such is his influence that many French wines are said to be *Parkerisés*: made to the powerful American's taste, namely big, bold and brassy with lashings of new oak.

Schist Type of flaky slate soil, good for growing vines.

Sommelier An intimidating wine waiter who looks at you as if you were something he might have stepped in.

Tannins Harsh, bitter, cheek-drying element in red wine derived from grape skins, pips and stems and from ageing in oak barrels. They taste like sucking a tea bag but soften over time. Essential if a wine is intended for ageing.

Toffee-nosed Description of wines that are slightly oxidised. Also applies to some wine writers.

Ullage The gap between the surface of the wine and the top of the bottle. It tends to increase as a wine ages.

Vin de table/vino da tavola Wine which will drink you under the table.

Vin de garde A wine intended for ageing.